Contents

Photographic credits
Unless otherwise specified all photographs are from the YSMA archive.

The Contributors

Charalambos Bouras, Professor Emeritus, President of the Committee for the Conservation of the Acropolis Monuments (ESMA)

Maria Ioannidou, civil engineer, Director of the Acropolis Restoration Service

Lena Lambrinou, MA, architect and archaeologist, The Parthenon Restoration Project, YSMA

Fani Mallouchou-Tufano, PhD, archaeologist, Professor of Technical University of Crete, member of ESMA

Dionysia Michalopoulou, civil engineer, Head of the Temple of Athena Nike restoration project

Evi Papakonstantinou-Ziotis, chemical engineer, Head of the surface conservation project

Tasos Tanoulas, PhD, architect, Head of the Propylaea restoration project

Nikos Toganidis, architect, Head of the Parthenon restoration project

Neil MacGregor

Director of the British Museum

Modern fascination for the civilization of ancient Greece is nowhere more powerfully focused than on the Acropolis of Athens. Its magnificent buildings have played a key role in the story of western architecture. Their influence is clearly visible in the British Museum which was built and decorated in Greek Revival style. When the British Museum's architect, Robert Smirke, was in Greece around 1800, the Acropolis monuments were confused with the ramshackle Ottoman village that had grown up around them. Following independence, Greece was quick to select the Acropolis as its national monument and the great buildings of pagan antiquity, cleared of all later accretions, were given new meaning as symbols of Greece ancient and modern.

Through the 19th and 20th centuries the ruinous condition of the monuments became an ever increasing matter of concern, not only in Greece but also abroad, as befits their status as world monuments. Eventually, progressive deterioration precipitated the restoration programme of the past 35 years. This has been an exemplary enterprise in every respect. It has been conducted in a remarkable spirit of openness and has been meticulous in setting new standards of good conservation practice.

In 1985 the British Museum staged an exhibition of the work that had been undertaken up until then by the Acropolis Ephorate and the Committee for the Conservation of the Acropolis Monuments. In October 2010, as the project drew to a close, the Museum hosted a study day at which the Acropolis Restoration team looked back over 35 years of conservation and shared some of the highlights with a London audience.

The papers are presented here in a joint publication by the British Museum and the Committee for the Conservation of Acropolis Monuments. The essays serve as a lasting testimony to the long-standing friendship that exists between colleagues on the Acropolis and the British Museum, a friendship that is steadily advancing our knowledge of the monuments. I wish to thank all those who took part in this happy event.

Lina Mendoni

Secretary General, Ministery of Culture and Tourism

A major conservation and restoration project on the Athenian Acropolis has been completed. The project started in 1975 with the creation of a special multidisciplinary Committee, the Committee for the Conservation of the Acropolis Monuments.

The restoration of the Erechtheum temple, which was brought to conclusion in 1987, was the first major intervention and it set the standards for what was to follow. A demanding technical project was combined with an extensive research programme. Technological innovation, scientific method and precision, theoretically informed choices, the employment of marble-carvers skilled in traditional techniques and, above all, teamwork were the hallmarks of this leading example of conservation of ancient Greek marble architecture. This first period also saw the launching of the restoration of the Propylaea and the completion of the programme of the east side of Parthenon, which have earned the acclaim of the international scientific community, as well as the appreciation of the general public.

In the year 2000 the newly established Acropolis Restoration Service undertook the continuation of the works already in progress on the Parthenon and the Propylaea, including the surface conservation of the ancient buildings and the inventorying of thousands of *membra disiecta*. In addition, a series of new projects were launched: notably the restoration of the temple of Athena Nike and the classical fortification walls. A radical reorganization of the whole enterprise, as well as generous funding by the European Union and the Greek State, resulted in the completion of this second phase this year.

The restored buildings have now acquired structural stability and offer the visitor a new perspective of the architectural ensemble that constituted the monumental entrance and the temples erected on the Sacred Rock in antiquity. Needless to say, that the end of the second phase does not connote the end of our obligations, nor of our commitment towards the continuous care for the site. Today a new programme is under way: the interventions on the pronaos, the opisthonaos and the north side of the temple now finalized, the restoration of the west side of the Parthenon is the next step. Meanwhile the transfer of the sculpted decoration to the New Acropolis Museum at the foot of the Rock and the exhibition of the entire collection originating from the excavations of the ancient site and the region that surrounds it create an enticing space of ancient and contemporary art and a place to study and contemplate the interweaving stories of ancient Athens and modern Europe.

The Parthenon and the Erechtheum in 2011

Introduction

Ian Jenkins

On the 8th October 2010 a Study Day was held at the British Museum, chaired by Lesley Fitton, Keeper of the Department of Greece and Rome. Its purpose was to survey and, at the same time, commemorate the 35-year long campaign of the restoration of the Acropolis monuments that was then nearing its end. All the speakers on that remarkable day were distinguished members of the Restoration team, some of whom had passed the greater part of their careers in dedicated service to the conservation and reconstruction of the Acropolis monuments.

First to speak was Professor Emeritus, Charalambos Bouras, President of the Committee for the Conservation of the Acropolis Monuments and presiding genius of the entire project without whose knowledge, enthusiasm and sense of purpose it would never have been completed. In recognition of his leadership of the Acropolis project and his substantial contribution to the study of Byzantine architecture, Professor Bouras was subsequently awarded honourary Fellowship of the London Society of Antiquaries. Professor Bouras was accompanied at the conference by his wife, Cornelia Hadziaslani, who has herself considerably increased public understanding of the Acropolis monuments through her own work as Head of the Education Department of the Acropolis Restoration Service.

Next to speak was Maria Ioannidou, Director of the Acropolis Restoration Service, whose tireless application of her many professional skills combined with her great warmth and generosity of spirit has greatly enriched the lives of all those who have been privileged to work with her. The next speaker, Tasos Tanoulas, has dedicated his working life to the Acropolis and to one monument in particular, the Propylaea of Mnesicles. Few architectural historians have the privilege of not only writing the history of a monument, but also of determining how it will look for years to come. The restoration of the ceiling coffers and of the interior Ionic colonnade have rendered the building substantially more coherent and given back to the architecture some of its former grandeur.

The next speaker was Dionysia Michalopoulou, who with great daring and professional skill took on and successfully delivered the reconstruction of the Nike temple. It is the third time that this temple has been rebuilt and this conscientiously correct renovation must surely be the last. In contrast with the exquisite diminutive of the Nike temple's Ionic order, Dr Nikos Toganides introduced the colossal Doric of the Parthenon. He served for many years under the charismatic direction of Professor Manolis Korres, and latterly he himself has led the Parthenon project. Toganides focused upon the east porch and on the north colonnade where Kostas Zambas had prepared the initial structural report which had warned alarmingly of imminent collapse. The audience especially appreciated the speaker's understated accounts of brilliant solutions of the restoration team for repositioning column drums misplaced during the previous restoration. Lena Lambrinou spoke next and presented a fascinating account of the intellectual as well as the material history of the north colonnade. This also provided a cultural history of the Acropolis at large.

The team of conservators responsible for the treatment of the marble surface of all the monuments was led by Evi Papakonstantinou. Besides detailing the painstaking conservation of the monuments over so many years, she graciously mentioned a recent collaboration between the Acropolis and the British Museum following the Museum's development of a photographic technique for detecting Egyptian blue pigment. This has lain invisible and undetected hitherto on the surface of marbles in Athens and in London. Finally Fani Mallouchou-Tufano, former Archivist of the project, looked back upon its early days and in particular the conservation of the Erechtheum. Fani paid homage to those like Alekos Papanikolaou who are no longer with us but whose great legacy endures. She also spoke eloquently and at times emotionally of the workers who are not always remembered by name but whose contribution to the success of the project is beyond measure

These published papers join a library of works that have been produced by the Committee for the Conservation of Acropolis Monuments. Much of this documentation is associated with a series of conferences and exhibitions which have been presented by the Committee as part of the admirable policy of openness.

The restoration has clothed the monuments in scaffolding and filled the terraces of the sacred rock with temporary workshops and offices. These have been staffed by architects, engineers, conservators and workers who have made the Acropolis so welcoming a place. Many and happy have been the days that I myself have spent going from one to another monument, visiting each in turn, to be greeted by colleagues who were never too busy to answer a question or share some new discovery.

The conference in 2010 was threatened by transport strikes in Athens in what has since become an increasingly serious financial crisis for Greece. Many of those whose names are mentioned here have had their formal employment affected by these developments and some have taken early retirement. The honour that they have earned and the benefit of their work to the monuments and generations of visitors to come can never be diminished. Their legacy will endure.

British Museum
Department of Greece and Rome

Thirty-five Years of Restoration of the Acropolis Monuments

Charalambos Bouras

Thirty-five years have elapsed since research into the Acropolis monuments, with a view to their restoration, first began (**Fig. 1**). The task of restoration took longer than expected. When the collective body in charge of the restoration was established in 1975 no one could have imagined that the project would take so long for the simple reason that no one had any in-depth knowledge of the existing problems. As it turned out, knowledge fostered need.

The urgency of that need was self-evident in instances where marbles had fallen from the Propylaea and the Parthenon and shattered. (**Fig. 2**). Such events indicated that previous attempts at restoration had been marked by serious miscalculations. Another source of concern was the surface erosion clearly visible on the marble which pointed to pollution in the atmosphere of Athens caused by carbon emissions.

This enormous intervention into the classical monuments of the Acropolis (**Fig. 3**) was a salvage operation made necessary and attenuated by the circumstances. Systematic examination of the ancient monuments constantly brought to our attention one form of damage after another. Just two years into the project, it became clear that, from antiquity to the present, the buildings had never been systematically maintained. The 5th-century AD repairs of the Parthenon following a ravaging fire were rather makeshift. Their sole purpose was to enable the building to resume its function as a temple.

Subsequent attempts at restoration from the time of Greece's independence to 1933 sought only to improve the outer appearance of the monuments by ridding them of later additions or by restoring the exterior. As a result of the ancient fire, the earthquakes, the 1687 explosion, and the 19th-century bombardments, the Parthenon suffered an alarming number of deep and shallow cracks that went unnoticed at the outset.

Thus, the restoration of the Parthenon, the Propylaea, and the Erechtheum did not remain confined to the mere replacement of the rusted metal elements left behind from Nicholaos Balanos' restorations from 1895–1933. They went on to include the structural restoration of the monuments. The works involved were exacting and precise as befits the preservation of all complex works of art. Consequently, they were time consuming.

During the 35 years spent researching, studying or accomplishing routine works on the monuments, many specialists in different fields joined and left the project team, while ideas and methods of restoration also came and went. Consequently, it is perhaps time for commentary or critique on the dynamics of the ethics governing the management of, as well as the intervention on the architectural legacy of the Acropolis and on the technical means available to us at present (**Fig. 4**).

The inter-scientific Committee for the Conservation of the Acropolis Monuments was established in 1975 by the late Minister of Culture, Constantinos Trypanis who, apart from being a professor emeritus of Greek Literature at Oxford University, was also a poet and an intellectual. Fully aware of the responsibility it had assumed in intervening in western architecture's pre-eminent monuments, the Committee mapped out a plan of action. It set the priorities for the different monuments, formulated the principles on the basis of which the interventions would take place and last but not least, established a technical office staffed with young engineers and archaeologists who were to define the necessary projects and then go on to implement them and oversee the works.

The Greek state shouldered the cost of the project as late as 1996 with the intention of preserving 'national value'. This is in keeping with the sentimental value that Greeks have attached

Figure 1 The Acropolis from the west

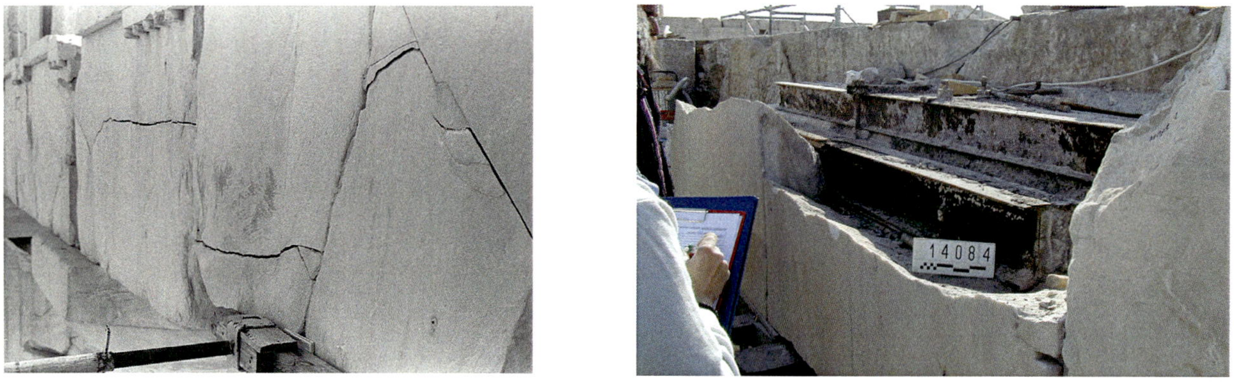

Figure 2 The entablature of the north colonnade of the Parthenon, showing fracturing from the swelling of metal components

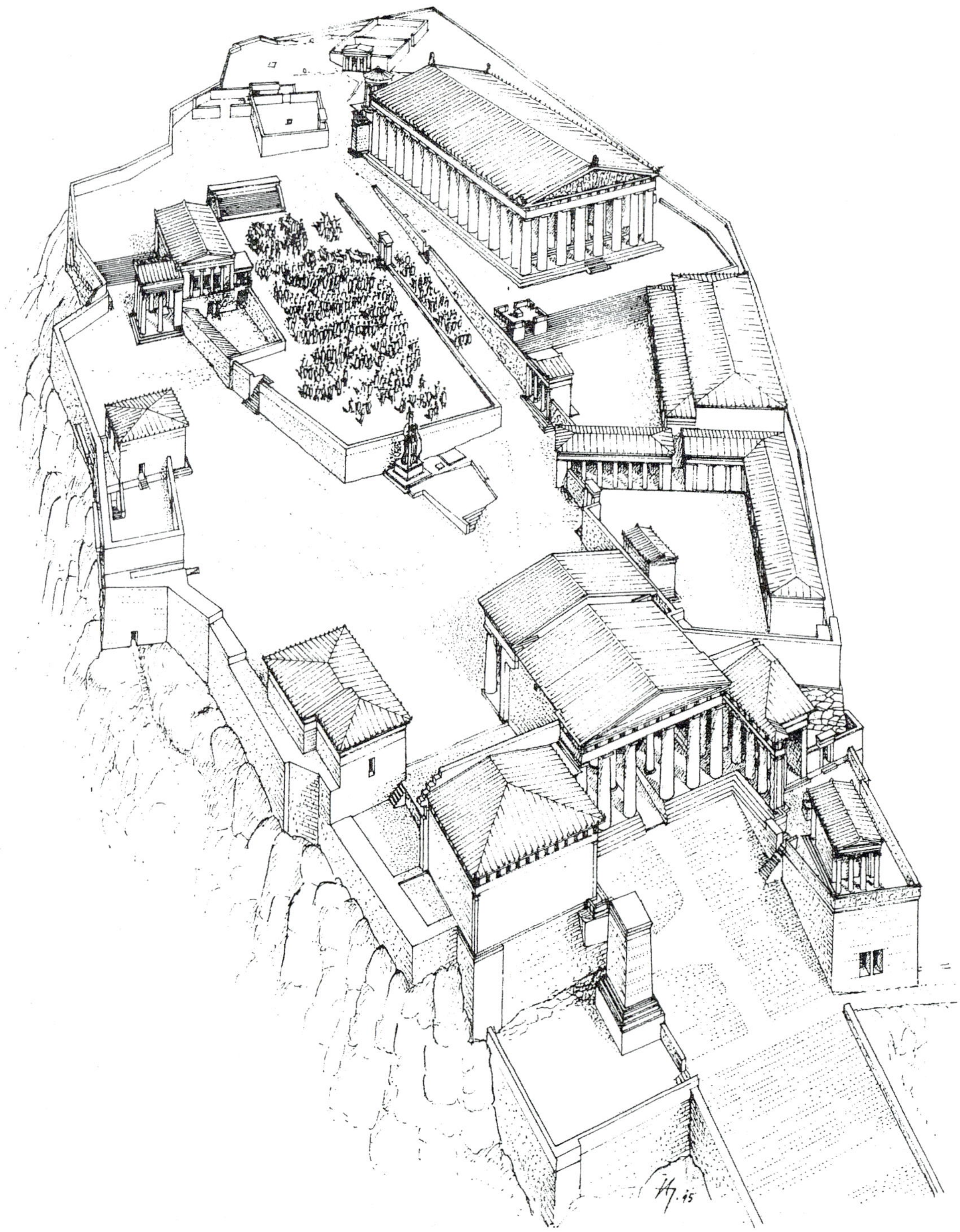

Figure 3 Drawing of the Acropolis, restored (G.P. Stevens)

Figure 4 The Acropolis from the south

to the Classical monuments of the country since the early 19th century. The intention to preserve and promote them constitutes one of the tenets governing the formulation of a national cultural identity and the concept of historic continuity in Greek society. The status of the Athenian monuments as national symbols and the admiration they attract internationally, exposed in a wealth of literature, indicate that similar views prevail in the wider European community as well.

The formulation of these principles that were destined to be deployed during the interventions on the Acropolis took place in 1975 and was accompanied by the relevant literature. As is well known, these tenets correspond to the values attributed by many societies to cultural artefacts. The first systematically to analyse the 'cult of monuments' was Alois Riegl in 1903 who clarified what those values were. Alois Riegl's views have never become outdated; they were recently translated and published again.

The Acropolis project has also paid particular attention to the international Venice Charter of 1964: its articles decree that historic, archaeological, artistic, and functional considerations together with environmental values, must be preserved. Along general lines, the Charter's articles correspond to Riegl's own analysis of values. Other rules came to be added in response to the value and nature of ancient Greek monuments and of those on the Acropolis in particular.

Reversibility, that is to say the capacity for returning an architectural member to its former state, prior to an intervention, was first and foremost based on a thorough respect for ancient material exposed not least through its detailed documentation. Another principle was that of respect for the ancient structure: it became mandatory to place marble blocks back in the original and only in their original position. It was also determined that each architectural member would remain independent should it become necessary to complement it with new marble parts. Architectural members that had erroneously been put together during previous restorations, because at the time they had seemed to belong together, had to be set to rights (**Fig. 5**). The Committee also determined that the monuments would keep their ruinous character with interventions restricted to what was absolutely necessary for them to regain support without excessive additions of new material. In other words, it was determined that new marble would be added only in its complementary role as structural material to certain members or would be used in order to build new ones on condition that the new ones also bore authentic ancient architectural members.

The Committee strives constantly to show transparency in its works not only with careful documentation of every modification made on the monuments but also in the theoretical basis of its decisions. Analytical minutes are always recorded of its meetings and an archive contains reports of those responsible for the various works, journals and related publications. Transparency was the primary reason for holding the five international meetings in 1977, (**Fig. 6**) 1983, 1989, 1994

Figure 5 Erechtheum after restoration

Figure 6 The first International Meeting of specialists for the preservation and restoration of the Acropolis monuments (1977)

and 2002. These landmark conferences brought together specialists who could learn of the progress made and discuss the principles on which restoration decisions are made. This same transparency also informed the exhibitions on the restorations that were held in London, Moscow, Paris, Amsterdam, Osaka, Rome, Berlin, Heidelberg, Freiburg, Sidney and Beijing. In the framework of information and education the Committee organized educational programmes for instructing mainly the young about the ancient art and architecture of the Acropolis.

At the outset our intention was to limit ourselves to the salvage operations necessary to allow the overall picture of the monuments to remain unaltered as it had been for decades. We wanted the monuments to look as they had after Balanos' restoration project. It should be noted also, that, later, the principles set out for the Acropolis were applied to other intervention projects around Greece which involved Classical monuments: in Epidaurus (**Fig. 7**), at Olympia, on Naxos, in the Athens Asklepieion (**Fig. 8**), and elsewhere.

During the 35 year-long campaign a mass of experience was accumulated. It was a time that saw the development of international relations and a growth in prosperity. The rapid progress in mass media and an increase in foreign travel brought about a significant shift in Greece's social values. There arose a new demand for popular culture and for broader understanding of cultural goods. The employment of the monuments (even in the form of exhibits) in generating economic growth through tourism, had become predominant. At the same time, new, international charters of ethics regarding monuments became accepted such as that of Cultural Tourism (Brussels 1976); the Treaty of Granada (1985); the European Treaty for the Protection of Archaeological Heritage (1992); and, in particular, the 'Recommendations for the Maintenance and Structural Restoration of Architectural Heritage'.

All such charters and treaties promote ethics which either do not conflict with the principles set out and adhered to by the Committee when dealing with the Acropolis project or they entail issues that are not relevant to the project. Nevertheless, the social trends of the past 35 years, together with wiser counsel, brought about certain amendments to our initial, more rigid specifications. More importantly, they brought about an extension of the old *anastelosis*. Thus, it was acknowledged that (a) the best way of preserving the architectural members lying on the ground, intact and damaged alike, was to incorporate them with the monuments that still stood; (b) the existing capabilities offered by systematic research into the members and the project site's infrastructure presented a unique opportunity to upgrade the monuments. More importantly (c), thorough understanding of the monuments had become a civic responsibility in order to demonstrate their artistic value, link them to the art education of citizens and reaffirm collective memory.

The literal meaning of the word *anastelosis* is: recomposing the whole through the exclusive use of architectural members that are no longer in their rightful place (**Fig. 9**). Such a task is usually not viable. In order to implement restoration, the addition of new materials must first become acceptable and, to the point where this is feasible, the extent of such additions must be confined. In *anastelosis* it is desirable to achieve balance between original and new materials; important too is the imperative to maintain the ruined character of the monument, even after the new additions have been implemented.

Figure 7 Epidaurus; the propylon of the palaestra after recent restoration (2009). Committee of the Epidauros Restoration archive

Figure 8 The Doric stoa of the Athenian Asklepieion, after restoration (2006). Committee of the Asklepieion Restoration archive

Figure 9 The Acropolis from the west

The most significant restoration after 1985 involved the Parthenon's pronaos (the porch in front of the cella). It was based on studies that Professor Manolis Korres had carried out for years. After the explosion of 1687, all that had been left from the eastern, inner six-pillared prostasis of the temple was a single column and the lower two or three drums of the remaining five. Yet, there were still more column drums which lay on the ground together with two full architraves. The four choices for resolving the problem presented by the pronaos were thoroughly discussed not only among Committee members but by numerous experts as well, during the International Meeting held in Athens in 1989. Finally, the consensus was to restore two columns to their full height and three more to a lesser height. The work involved has already been carried out and all that is now left is to carve the flutes in the new marble additions.

In the case of the Erechtheum it was decided to give it the form it had before 1805 by adding to its eastern colonnade the copy of an Ionic column which was removed by Lord Elgin and is in the British Museum (**Fig. 10**). The copy was made from artificial stone, which was moulded so that in terms of form no difference would be discerned between the new column and the original one. The plan of the Erechtheum, unique among ancient Greek temples with its four façades, all very different from each other, required that the main façade of the temple should appear as a complete form so that it would be comprehensible (legible if you wish) even if a copy were added. Copies of the Caryatids were also made in artificial stone (**Fig. 11**) since it had become imperative that the original statues be moved to a protected indoor space. Today, the Caryatids are on display in the new Acropolis Museum (**Fig. 12**).

Figure 10 Erechtheum; the east prostasis after restoration (1979–87)

Figure 11 Erechtheum; cast copies of the Caryatids in the south porch, after restoration

Figure 13 Propylaea; the central building, looking up to the restored coffered ceiling

Let us now turn to the Propylaea, Mnesicles' monumental gateway to the Acropolis. Around 1900 Balanos had restored one of the 12 sections of the marble roof, which had been famous even in antiquity. Finding, identifying, and assembling hundreds of fragments from the roof coffers led to the opportunity to restore yet another of the roof's 12 sections, by the addition of new marble to the beams supporting the coffer-slabs (**Fig. 13**). The artistic impression of the Propylaea's eastern stoa was enhanced by means of also integrating earlier coffer-slabs. On the southern side of the stoa, the Doric entablature was restored by employing ancient architectural members.

The marble floor of the temple of Athena Nike was restored and the eastern pediment received minor additions to its cornices (**Fig. 14**).

It has often been said of this series of restorations that the result is a form of the monument never seen before in the course of its history. That is true and it also holds true for many of the ancient monuments and those on the Acropolis in particular: the Parthenon; the Propylaea; and the temple of Athena Nike. Our abiding aim has been to ensure that the new appearance of the ruined buildings, wherever possible,

Figure 12 Acropolis Museum; the original Caryatid statues on display (Photo: Acropolis Museum)

Figure 14 The temple of Athena Nike after the restoration

Figure 15 Parthenon; restored columns of the pronaos, before fluting of the drums

Figure 16 The coffered marble slabs, carved (1960 – 62) in order to cover the west wing of the Parthenon peristasis

incorporates the ancient members formerly scattered on the ground. This helps to evoke the monuments' initial form. At the same time, this new appearance is vindicated by its own inner economy. Furthermore it is a testimony to contemporary scientific research and practice which made the restoration possible (**Fig. 15**).

Another issue contingent on the above is the problem of the marble coffer-slabs carved during the 1950s in order to cover the Parthenon's west porch. (**Fig. 16**) Since the ancient beams were still in place, the thinking was to restore these coffers in order to protect in situ the temple's west frieze. Now that the west frieze blocks are housed in the Museum, installing those panels today would only serve in protecting the temple's west stoa from rain or frost. At the time of my writing these coffer-slabs are almost 60 years old. Their inclusion in the restored Parthenon would significantly increase the quantity of new marble that would have to be added to the monument. The issue has yet to be resolved.

The rapid pace of technology from 1975 to the present has greatly improved the working methods employed on the Acropolis. Computer applications and digital photography have significantly facilitated the daily documentation of the project's works prior to and during the interventions. At the same time, they have allowed the classification and indexing of documented drawings, photographs, videos, logs, and studies in a database which has a wide range of uses. By means of a 3-D scanner directly linked to a pantograph, contemporary technology has facilitated the carving of the joining surface between original and replacement part of architectural members. Their technology also produces orthophotographs of great precision, (**Fig. 17**) invaluable in analysing structural problems.

For all the benefits of their technology there has been no corresponding progress in materials. There is, for example, the need for a material that can be applied to marble surfaces to protect them against acid rain, while at the same time transparent and reversible. So far, no such material exists.

Figure 17 Orthophotomosaic of the south circuit wall of the Acropolis

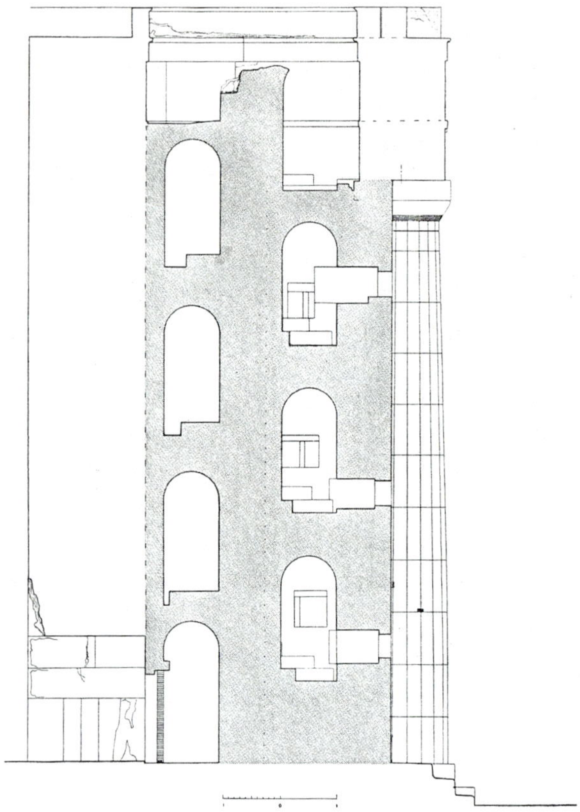

Figure 18 The Byzantine staircase on the south-west corner of the Parthenon cella. (Drawing: the author)

Still, the issue does not have the gravity it had in 1975, since the new generation of domestic fuels used in Athens no longer pollutes the atmosphere through the emission of sulphur dioxide. This once was the most alarming threat looming over the Acropolis monuments.

In the 35 years that have gone by, there has been a steady decrease of interest in artistic works which involve manual labour. This has become noticeable even in contemporary art. One of the problems of the Acropolis project is recruiting marble carvers who are as skilled as ancient carvers in carving the marble and as adept at manoeuvring architectural members of great weight. This problem is being gradually resolved thanks to the tutelage the younger technicians receive in the hands of the older ones. Regrettably, the same claim cannot be made by fellow architects who use computers to draw their plans, a technique which sadly strips their work of its artistic value which has always been an intrinsic part of architectural plans and drawings.

During the 19th and 20th centuries, the infinite admiration for ancient Greece and art in the age of Pericles became the cause for the systematic destruction of all medieval and modern-day edifices on the Acropolis. As a result, a significant archaeological site was deprived of all evidence relating to its modern history. This generated the fallacy that, all along, some lifeless ruins have been standing there on their own. In other words, 'diachronic stratification' on the Acropolis has been lost with the exception of the Byzantine staircase of the Parthenon's belfry (**Fig. 18**). The restoration of the small monopterae temple of Rome and Augustus east of the Parthenon (**Fig. 19**) may perhaps become, during some future restoration project,

Figure 19 In the mid-ground, ruins of the monopteral temple of Roma and Augustus, on the Acropolis

Figure 20 Orthophotomosaic view of the Acropolis (2009) showing the temporary installations supporting the works. (YSMA archives)

living proof of the history of the Acropolis, at least, during the Roman era.

Furthermore, another problem awaiting resolution is the Acropolis monuments' environment itself in relation to Acropolis visitors. The old archaeological excavations stripped the rock of its fillings, removing all soil that was instrumental in shaping the earlier levels of the ground. The problem was compounded in the last 30 years by the addition of installations necessary to the project (**Fig. 20**): cranes, scaffolding, workshops; shelters, storage space, etc. To a great extent, these installations concealed the monuments from view and greatly restricted the free space necessary for the visitors to move about and to enjoy a view of the monuments as well as of the surrounding urban vista of Athens. A study by Professor Manolis Korres, which saw the light in 2002, points out that the levels of the Acropolis ground must be restored, once the project has been completed and the present installations have been removed. Only then we will be able to say with any certainty that the works on the Athenian Acropolis have truly come to an end.

Research and Technology

Maria Ioannidou

The use of contemporary technology for the restoration of historical monuments along with traditional techniques and methods is included among the principles of the Venice Charter. This is the first internationally accepted theoretical framework of principles for interventions on historical monuments. In recent years, perceptions stemming from globalization require the use of modern technology for the protection of the monuments. Advanced technology is utilized more and more during the research and performance phase of the programme of protection (**Fig. 1**). The primary concern is to repair the structure and form and to display historical and artistic values they embody.

Advanced technology in study, research, and the execution of the works, has been a basic characteristic of the interventions on the Acropolis monuments. This was so from the very beginning in 1975 and the founding of ESMA, the Committee for the Conservation of the Acropolis Monuments. After 2000 and the establishment of the Acropolis Restoration Service (YSMA), by the Ministry of Culture, advanced technology supported the development and acceleration of the extensive restoration programme and led to innovative scholarly and technical methods and to technological applications.

Interventions on the monuments from 1975 onwards were considered inevitable; serious structural damage was caused mainly by the choices of a previous restoration, while problems of surface erosion stemmed from the atmospheric pollution. The identification of the marble architectural members that lay scattered on the Acropolis Rock, their re-setting in the monuments from which they come and the correction of the faulty placing of marble members in the previous interventions led to a broader *anastelosis*, extended to a greater part of the monuments, thus increasing their comprehensibility and their educational value. This theoretical framework was the basis for the methodology that was followed in the restoration work.

So it was that the marble blocks of the monuments, previously restored, had to be dismantled. The dismantling was extended to sections that had not been restored in the past

Figure 1 The Acropolis during restoration

Figure 2 Dismantling the column capital of the Propylaea west hall

Figure 3 Mending joining fragments of an architrave block of the north side of the Parthenon with titanium rods

Figure 4 Fitting a new marble filling to a column capital of the north colonnade of the Parthenon

but showed signs of deterioration. The rusted joining elements of the previous restoration were removed and the filling material – cement plaster in the restored areas or, rarely lead – was taken out (**Fig. 2**).

White cement and titanium reinforcements are used for the structural restoration of the architectural members; threaded titanium rods were inserted into holes in the marble mass and secured by an inorganic plaster that was made of white cement. Titanium is used as a connecting element for joining fragments of architectural members (**Fig. 3**). It is a relatively light metal, of satisfactory strength and with features (the coefficient of thermal expansion and the modulus of elasticity) that allow it to work well with marble. The main characteristic for which it was chosen for connecting the members, however, is its excellent resistance to all forms of corrosion. Fragments that do not belong together, that is to say, that do not come from the same architectural member, are never joined together.

Where necessary, missing parts have been added in new marble so that they have regained their original form and structural independence (**Fig. 4**). The new marble fillings are usually limited and the criterion for the decision is always structural efficiency of the member and of the monument, and the structural and aesthetic autonomy of the areas being restored. The aim is not to rebuild the monument, but to preserve the character of the ruin and whatever bears witness to its course through history. The additions to the blocks are of Pentelic marble from the Dionysos quarries. The joining surfaces of the additions are cut with the use of a pointing device for copying named *pontadoros* or an electric pantograph. Both methods ensure that the additions agree precisely with the broken surface of the ancient block being filled in. The additional pieces are joined to the ancient marble pieces with titanium rods and a special cement compound.

Then, the eroded surface of the monuments undergoes surface conservation, a work comprising the consolidation of disintegrating surfaces, the filling of cracks with injected mortar and the removal of soot deposit and black crust (**Figs 5a-b**).

Figures 5a-b Erechteum , block of the west wall. Condition of the surface before and after conservation

Figure 6 Parthenon; resetting of an architrave of the north colonnade

Figure 7 Resetting of the titanium clamps in the ancient cuttings

Figure 8 Parthenon; lowering an ancient metope from the north side of the monument

When the architectural members have been repaired, they are set again in their original positions or in positions found after research. In exceptional cases where this is not possible the architectural members are set in the position they held in the previous restoration.(**Fig. 6**). They are connected with titanium elements - clamps and dowels - which are secured in the ancient clamp and dowel cuttings and sockets with inorganic plaster according to the ancient system of joining (**Fig. 7**). In designing the clamps and dowels, the aim is that the weaker element of the join should be the metal clamp or dowel. Thus in case of great stress the joint can withstand permanent deformation and, if deemed necessary, there can be a new intervention, limited to replacing the metal elements.

During the re-setting of members, geometrical deformations of the area that was dismantled are partially corrected to the extent allowed by the remaining distortions of the members that were not dismantled, in order to achieve as much as possible the original form.

Finally, in order to avoid irreversible damage, the architectural sculptures are moved to the Acropolis Museum (**Fig. 8**); they are replaced on the monuments by accurate copies in artificial stone, finished especially for tone and texture (**Fig. 9**).

Figure 9 Parthenon *opisthonaos*; view of west frieze. The original blocks of the west frieze are replaced by copies of artificial stone

A big restoration project started in 2001, funded by the Hellenic State and the European Community, with restoration works to the Parthenon, the masterpiece of ancient Greek architecture, the little Ionic temple of Athena Nike and the Propylaea, the monumental entrance to the sanctuary on the Rock (**Fig. 10**). This project comprising also the recording and listing of the thousands of ancient stones scattered on the Acropolis plateau as well as the monitoring and consolidating of the circuit walls around the Acropolis slopes, was brought to completion in 2010 (**Fig. 11**). The restoration of the Erechtheum was completed in 1987.

During the last decade – from 2001 to 2010 – more than 1,094 blocks of the monuments with a weight of 2,675 tons have been dismantled, mended and restored; 686 blocks were joined from fragments; 905 fillings were made from new marble, while 158 blocks were carved from new marble. For this enormous project almost 530m^3 of new marble were used.

Figure 10 The Acropolis from the Pnyx after completion of the restoration of 2001-2010

Figure 11 The Acropolis from Lykabettos after completion of the restoration 2001-2010

During the restoration works, much new information has come to light about the archaeology, history and architecture of the Acropolis monuments, while in these fields the monuments are – and will continue to be – the focus of study by leading scholars. The new information has not simply increased our knowledge and added to the relevant bibliography; it has contributed to the compiling of studies that are basic to the interventions being carried out. Yet, theoretical, scholarly and technical problems have been encountered during the application of these studies. To resolve those problems, research has been carried out by the scholarly personnel of the works, either alone or in collaboration with educational institutions or other Greek research centres and Institutions as the National Technical University of Athens, the Institute of Technology and Research of Crete, the National Observatory of Athens, the nuclear research centre Democritos among others.

Within the framework of the academic and scholarly research undertaken in the recent years, the most important interventions could be listed as follows.

Research on the joining of ancient fragments scattered on the Rock and the forming of architectural members from fragments found on the ground. This work, along with the identification of the original position of the members, allows greater areas of the monuments to be restored.

A representative example is the restoration of the ceilings of the Propylaea with coffered slabs and beams, over a surface that is almost double that of the previous restoration (**Fig. 12**). The intervention provided the opportunity for a systematic research of more than 1,000 fragments that came both from dismantling and from the ceiling fragments that lay scattered on the ground and that had not been used in the previous restoration. The fragments were grouped and separated with the help of a computer according to their various characteristics such as the dimensions, the quality of work on the surface of the fragments, the quality of the marble, the geological layering, existence of interior marble discontinuities (*kommoi*), colour and texture, the traces left from the earlier intervention on the coffers. The method, using also optical drawings of the break surfaces, was especially successful for joining fragments and re-creating coffered slabs. The research led to fragments belonging together that with small additions of new marble, formed architectural members of the ceilings. These comprised coffered slabs and beams that could be restored in their original position or in similar positions in the ceilings. (See also the contribution of T. Tanoulas in this volume.)

Rearrangement of certain areas of the monuments, restored in the past, by resetting architectural members in their correct positions, on the basis of new evidence found after their dismantling.

The criteria for the research were: measurements of the dimensions of the blocks to millimetre precision; the quality of the marble; the geological layering; the existence of interior marble discontinuities (*kommoi*), colour and texture; the quality of work on the surface of the fragments, as well as deterioration features on the marble surface; special architectural and construction details.

Among the representative examples of the above should be mentioned: the rearrangement of 6 blocks of the south and 23 blocks of the north walls of the Erechtheum (see also the contribution of F. Mallouchou-Tufano in this volume); the restoration of the north colonnade of the Parthenon (**Fig. 13**) after resetting the drums in their original position (see also the contribution of N. Toganidis and L. Lambrinou in this volume); the rearrangement of the wall blocks of the temple of Athena Nike (see also the contribution of D. Michalopoulou in this volume).

Figure 12 Ceilings of the west hall and the east stoa of the Propylaea after restoration

Figure 13 Parthenon; north side after restoration

The structural restoration of architectural members and development of an original calculating method for joining marble fragments with titanium reinforcements, according to the strain applied to the members.

The titanium reinforcements are calculated so as to take on tensile force in a direction at right angles to the surfaces of fracture. The basic criterion for calculating the reinforcements is that they can safely take on the functional loads and in a near limit situation the reinforcements in the joining should fail rather than the marble itself (**Fig. 14**). During recent years, special emphasis has been attached to the method of restoring the monolithic aspect of the large bending members of the monuments (beams and architrave blocks). This is developing continuously, from the standpoint of both calculation and process of application in the work site.

The structural efficiency against static or dynamic charges, of the restored areas of the monuments and of those *in situ*.

This research was carried out in collaboration with other scientific bodies developing the study of natural and mechanical properties of the building materials of the monuments and the materials used in the restoration, such as ancient and new marble, ancient iron, titanium, special mortars.

The behaviour of the parts reinforced by titanium has been studied in bending trials and pull-out tests. The behaviour of beams mended with titanium rods is also being studied in three-point bending tests. These tests are particularly important for the restoration of large bending members (beams, epistyles).

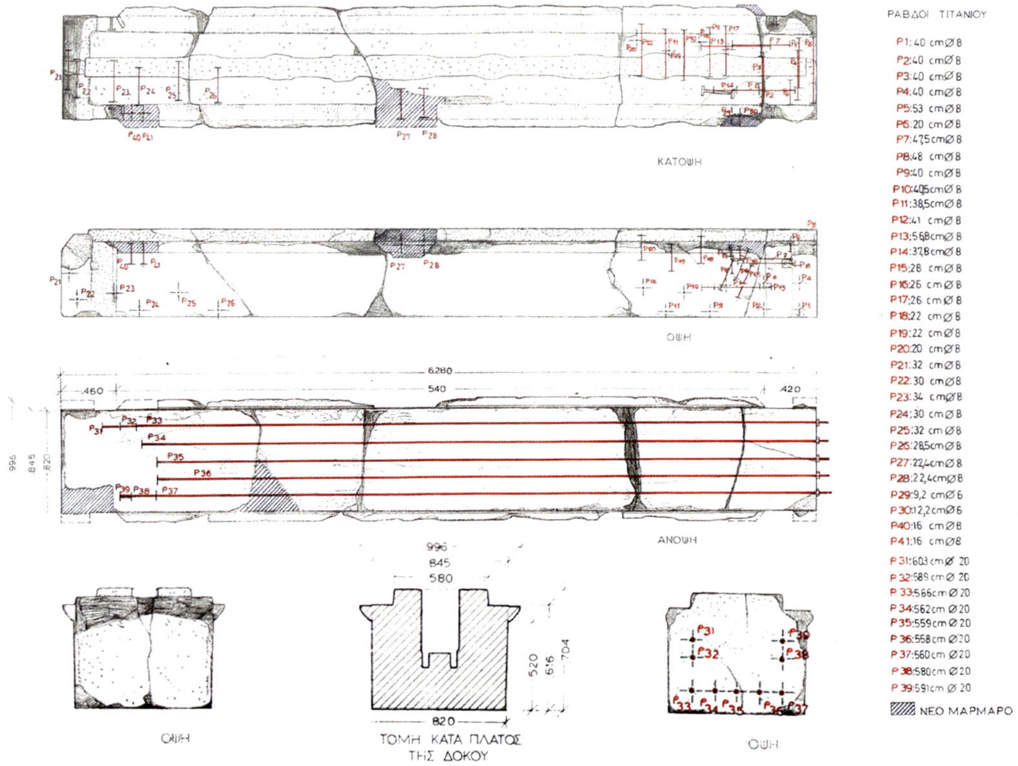

Figure 14 Propylaea, east stoa. Structural restoration of a beam with titanium rods. (Study and drawing: M. Ioannidou)

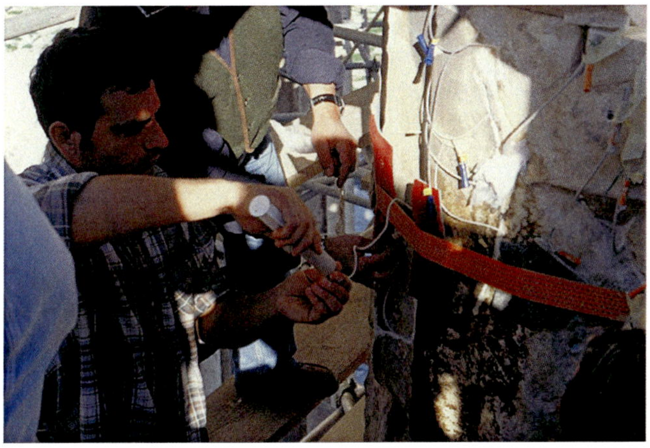

Figure 15 Parthenon opisthonaos; repairing *in situ* the cracks of the columns

Figure 16 The ancient crane of the Parthenon. (Drawing: M. Korres)

Figure 17 Parthenon; dismantling a block from the west pediment using a special grab

Development of innovative applications during the course of the works. Representative examples are as follows.

1. The repair *in situ* of the cracks in columns of the Parthenon *opisthonaos* caused by thermal fracture in antiquity (**Fig. 15**). In order to avoid dismantling them and to retain their authentic structure, the cracks in the drums were injected with a hydraulic grout especially prepared for this pupose.
2. Innovative application is the method applied for the conservation and cleaning of the sculptured surface of the blocks of the Parthenon west frieze, dismantled in 1992, in order to repair the damage it had suffered during its long history on the monument. The cleaning of the blocks from the soot deposit and the black crust that had covered them was a most sensitive and delicate operation, since the historical layers of the surface of the sculpture had to be preserved. The cleaning method chosen was the laser in an entirely original application, using simultaneously two wavelengths, infrared and ultraviolet. By means of this system, the frieze blocks were safely cleaned without affecting the underlying layer. In addition the historical layers of the surfaces of the frieze were preserved, with an excellent aesthetic result; information about the original workmanship and traces of ancient colour were also revealed (see also the contribution of E. Papakonstaninou in this volume).
3. Special emphasis given during 2010, to the conservation and cleaning of the ceiling of the Porch of the Caryatids in the Erechtheum using this laser system. In the course of cleaning were revealed traces of painted decoration and traces of ancient paint. Apart from the application of non-destructive methods of analysis for the study and analysis of these traces, research on the Egyptian blue is being carried out in collaboration with the British Museum.

The development of important technical knowledge on hoisting systems that are used for dismantling and reassembling the monuments.

To a great extent this technological knowledge is based on ideas and hoisting systems already known and employed in antiquity for building the monuments (**Fig. 16**). Developments and achievements of modern technology, however, are utilized in the motive power of the systems and in the choice of material. Thus we have metal systems of cranes and scaffolding, which are moved by electricity with low speeds and can obtain great precision. Special care is taken with the form and extent of the hoisting system used, so that it is adaptable to the particular aesthetic and environmental requirements of the sensitive area of each monument, which is surrounded by ancient remains and at the same time must cope daily with hordes of visitors.

The tools employed in the *anastelosis* are about the same as those used by the ancient technicians for building the monuments. Innovative constructions, however, using the ultimate in modern technology were developed in order to accelerate the works, while retaining their well-known high quality.

As representative examples should be mentioned: grabs for lifting architectural members (**Fig. 17**), special pointing devices used for the construction of the missing parts of the

Figure 18 Parthenon; orthophotomosaic of the entablature and pediment of the west side. (Study: D. Mauromati)

Figure 19 Orthophotomosaic of the ground plan of the Erectheum

Figure 20 Orthophomosaic of the ground plan of the Ancient Temple.

marble blocks. Notable among these is the cutting machine, devised for carving the flutes of the column drums of new marble that can cut to millimetre precision. Its use has greatly accelerated the work of restoration of the North Colonnade of the Parthenon. The final phase of carving the flutes is to be done by hand by the experienced marble technicians of the Service.

The development of a specially designed original electronic database. Its purpose is to make available systematic documentation, graphic, photographic, cinematographic etc., which has been carried out from the very beginning of the work and accompanies all its phases.

In recent years special emphasis has been placed on using techniques of advanced technology for documenting and graphic mapping of the monuments, the fortification walls and the rock itself.

Geometric documentation is the first step in the restoration of a monument. What is of particular interest is the recording and mapping of the changes in the original geometry of the monument and the damage it has suffered. These features, in connection with the study of the historical and archaeological evidence and the structural pathology of the monument, form the necessary infrastructure for its restoration. In the case of the Acropolis, from 1975 on, the possibilities offered by the use of conventional methods and instruments were employed for surveying the monuments:

Among the applications of recent years an attempt was made to utilise photogrammetry, the science that uses information about natural objects and the environment drawn from the procedure of recording, measuring and interpreting photographic images.

The development of photogrammetry during the past years, with the application of digital techniques, has made it possible to produce orthophotomosaics and three-dimensional models of high quality and precision. With correct processing and composition of significant numbers of photographs, this method allows the production of orthophotomosaics that combine the geometrical accuracy of the plan with the optical-quality information of the photograph (**Fig. 18**).

In the framework of a large programme entitled 'Development of a Geographical Information System in the Acropolis of Athens', the following activities were accomplished during recent years:

1. Establishment of single geodetic networks.
2. Mapping of the relief of the Acropolis with full topographical and photogrammetric survey of the walls and a plan of the Acropolis (**Figs 19–20**).
3. Three-dimensional (3-D) scanning of the Erechtheum (**Figs 21a-b**) and the fortification walls for their full length, interior and exterior (**Figs 21a–b**).
4. Development of a flexible Geographical Information System (GIS), together with the upgrading of the existing database of the *anastelosis* interventions.
5. Export of all the data to the internet (www.ysma.gr).

Figures 21a-b Erechtheum. 3-D models of the Caryatids

Figure 22 Acropolis, north circuit wall, incorporating column drums of the pre-Parthenon

Of special interest is the study of the problems of the Acropolis circuit walls, a monument of exceptional importance.

The continuous repairs from antiquity to the present day have contributed to their survival. Even so, structural damage, such as cracks, gaps and severe deformations, is apparent in many areas of the ancient construction as well as in the parts comprising later repairs. The programme that is today in full development concerns the systematic monitoring of the Wall, in order to research its static efficiency, compile studies and carry out interventions on it of rescue nature (**Fig. 22**).

Among the applications of recent years, the most important are:

1 Geophysical prospection: electrical tomography was carried out in order to determine the contours of the south side of the Wall. It was not possible to determine precise geometric contours, but an area with a high amount of dampness was located.
2 Installation of a network of seven accelerographs at specific points of the Rock and the Parthenon. The purpose of developing this network, being carried out collaboration with the Geodynamic Institute of the National Observatory of Athens, is to record seismic action and the response of the hill and the monuments to these.
3 Installation of a system of optical fibres with sensors to detect deformations, temperature and pressure at specific points on the circuit Wall and the monuments.
4 Highly accurate measurements of topographical targets on the Wall. The measurements are for the purpose of monitoring micro-movements at specific points of the Wall with a topographical instrument of high accuracy.

Finally, we must report the recent activities of the YSMA that are intended, using advanced technology, to inform the scholarly world and the general public about the monuments and the works of anastelosis:

1 Creation of a 'Virtual Theatre' in the New Acropolis Museum. Shown in that gallery will be stereoscopic and simple projections of films about the history of the *anastelosis* of the four great monuments of the Acropolis.
2 Reforming the YSMA website .
3 Production of films with three-dimensional graphics. The YSMA has already made three films entitled 'The Acropolis in Antiquity', 'Building an Ancient Temple' and 'The *Anastelosis* of the Erechtheum'.
4 Installation of electronic information stations (infokiosks) on the Acropolis.

The completion of the great *anastelosis* programme, launched in 2001, brings to an end a highly productive period in the Acropolis restoration story. Special mention must be made of all the staff of the works; the scholarly, the technical, the support personnel, all of whom worked intensively in order to finish it. The collaboration, the group spirit, the good working environment, the feeling that we were sharing in the solving of the problems of the monuments reinforced our efforts.

Programmed for the coming years are interventions in other parts of the monuments that show structural problems. It is my belief that in the new phase of the works, the driving forces will be the knowledge and experience gained in the preceding years, together with the creative spirit and enthusiasm that has characterised the period that has ended.

The current restoration project on the Acropolis bears, as always, the stamp of its time. It responds to the contemporary social demands for a more direct comprehension, enjoyment and experience of the heritage from our ancestors. At the same time it reflects the advanced scientific and technological level and know-how not only of contemporary Greece but also of the whole European Community. The Acropolis restoration project is a European project not because it is partially financed by the European Union, but because it affects monuments that constitute the cradle of European thought, feeling and culture.

The Propylaea

Tasos Tanoulas

Monuments with a long history of use can be compared to palimpsests: they preserve traces of the successive phases of their purpose which the archaeologist must detect, identify and interpret. With such important buildings as those of the Acropolis of Athens there is yet one more phase, namely their restoration. The restorer is tasked to return the monument to its material, three-dimensional form in order to permanently represent its identity and project the past into the future. Practical, aesthetic and moral factors are involved. All these make the restoration of each monument an individual case.

Even in the case of the Acropolis, despite all the buildings sharing the same structural elements, the restoration of each individual building has its particular characteristics. This is due to the original design, the structural history and, in addition, to the fact that the interventions carried out in the first half of the 20th century under the direction of Nikolaos Balanos lasted for almost 40 years. During this long period of time not only the technology but also the philosophical concept of restoration changed considerably.

The Propylaea (**Fig. 1**) were built between 437 and 432 BC as part of the Periclean building project, which also included the Parthenon, the Erechtheum and the temple of Athena Nike. The Propylaea were never finished, and the building complex that was to be accomplished consisted of three parts. The central building had hexastyle Doric porticoes facing east and west and was divided into two unequal parts by a transverse wall, pierced with five doors. A ramp along the central axis was flanked, in the western hall, by three pairs of fine Ionic columns, supporting a ceiling of a magnificence unparalleled in antiquity. Two smaller Doric porticoes flanked the western front with their symmetrical, smaller Doric tristyle in antis colonnades; the northern one was the vestibule to a large room, the so-called Pinakotheke, while the southern one was a mere stoa leading to the sanctuary of Athena Nike. From the end of the 3rd century AD to 1833, the Propylaea were closely related to the fortification system of the western access to the Acropolis. The Byzantines used the northern wing as the residence of the Greek Metropolitan of Athens which, in the 13th century, was incorporated, by the French dukes of Athens, de la Roche, into their fortified residence; in the 15th century, the Florentine duke, Antonio Acciaiuoli, extended the residential area into the central building. In 1640, the explosion of gunpowder which had been stored by the Turkish occupants in the Propylaea destroyed a great part of the ceilings and the superstructure. Since then the building became dilapidated and further damaged, with the resultant extinction of most of the architectural parts of the superstructure (**Fig. 2**).

The first restoration of the Propylaea was conducted by Nikolaos Balanos between 1909–17. In the eastern portico, Balanos restored the architrave, more than half of the frieze

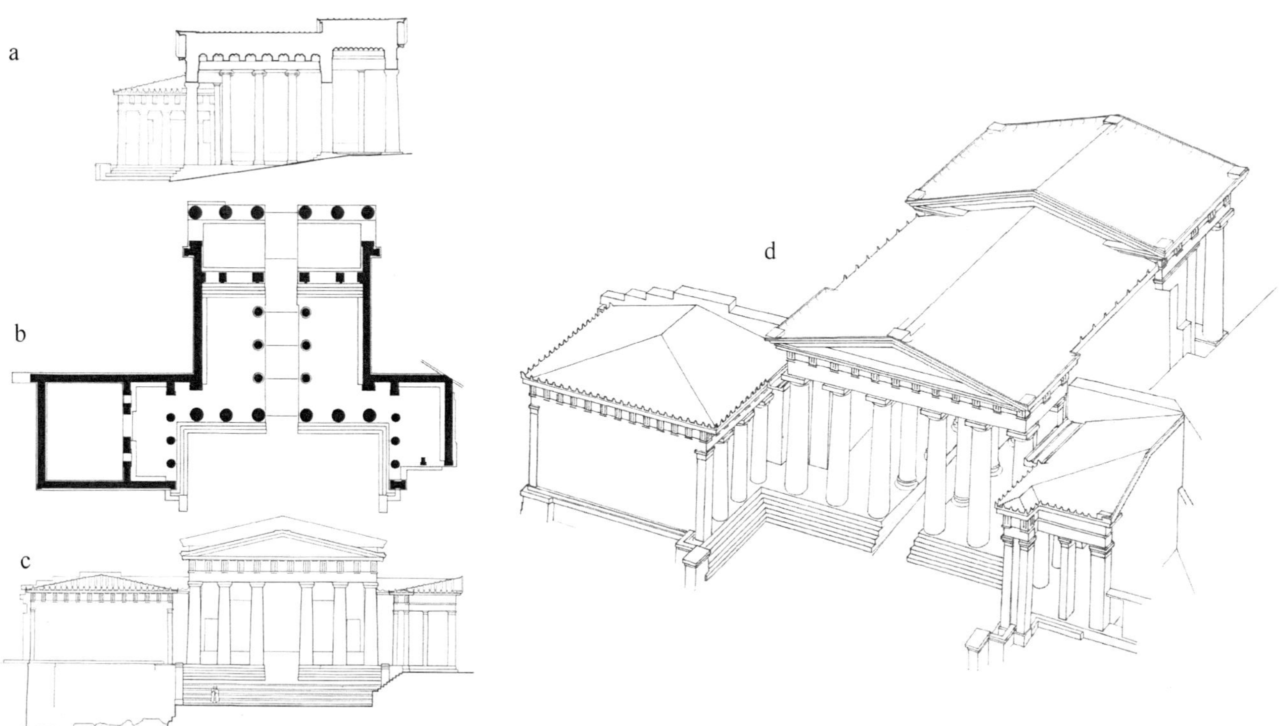

Figure 1 The Propylaia in antiquity. **a**: cross-section through the axis of the central building, looking north; **b**: Plan; **c**: Western façade; **d**: Aximetric view from the south-west

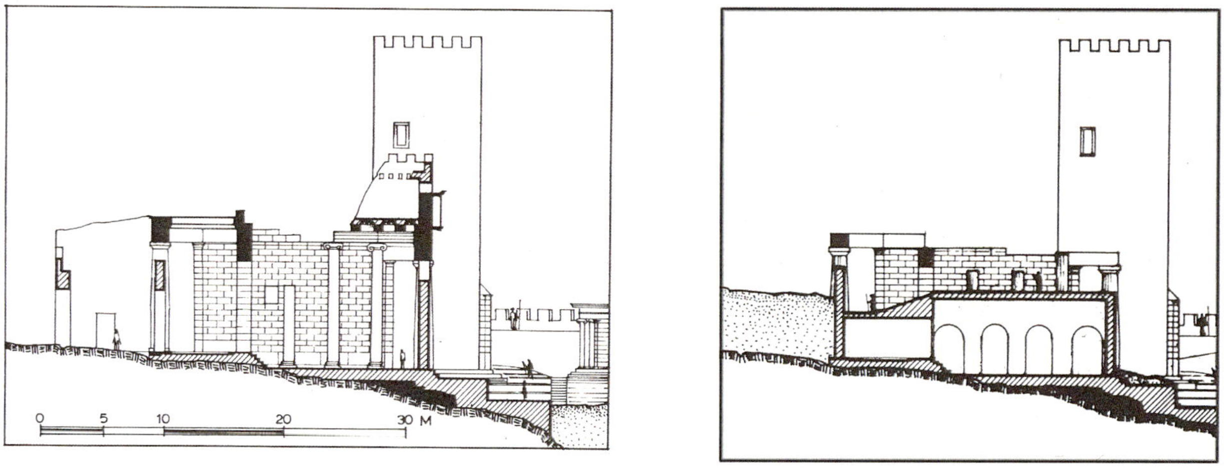

Figure 2 left: The Propylaea after the explosion in 1640; **right**: The Propylaea after the installation of the battery of cannon after 1700

Figures 3a-b The eastern portico of the Propylaea before and after Balanos' restorations. (Photos: Deutsches Archäologisches Institut; The Archaeological Society in Athens, Balanos archives)

Figures 4a-b Propylaea; removing parts of the ceilings restored by Balanos (1992). The technology used on the work-site allowed the quick removal of huge blocks from the top of the monument (**above**) to the ground (**below**)

and cornice, less than half of the pediment, as well as the northern end of the ceiling. In the western hall, he reassembled the extreme eastern column of the northern Ionic colonnade on which, successively, the north-east part of the ceiling was restored (**Fig. 3a-b**).

The ongoing project for the restoration of the Propylaea started in the years 1981–82, with the intervention in the fourth architrave of the east portico, counting from the north. The problem to be solved was, as in all the other monuments on the Acropolis, the destruction of the marble due to the oxidation of the iron used by Balanos. In 1989 the documented proposal for the dismantlement of the parts of the ceilings restored between 1909 and 1917 was presented at the International Meeting for the Restoration of the Acropolis Monuments and, later, to the Central Archaeological Board of Greece.

Before the intervention, it was necessary to build the substructure of the work-site. Owing to the location of the building at the west edge of the Acropolis plateau, and because of the vulnerable remains of poros buildings which surround the Propylaea, the only space available for the installation of the work site was the area to the northeast of the central building, where the Justinianian cistern, the pre-Mnesiclean cistern, and the so-called north-west building are located. The Justinianian cistern had to be emptied of the archaeological material that had been deposited there in 1890, at the end of the big Acropolis excavations (1885–90). Three hundred cubic metres of marble and poros blocks, together with rubble stone and soil, were extracted. The material was photographed and inventoried. The work site had to be organized on a platform raised on iron posts, causing no harm to the ancient relics below nor to the rock, which is regarded as a monument on its own.

After completion of the construction of the work site, the first task was to take down the parts of the coffer- ceilings restored at the north-east part of the central building. Between June 1990 and July 1993, all the beams, the coffer slabs, the inter-beam slabs, as well as the Ionic epistyle and capital restored in the west hall were taken down (**Fig. 4a-b**). Their condition, because of the fragmentation due to the oxidized iron, was lamentable. Our philosophy concerning the conservation of the dismantled parts dictated that, at this stage of the work, only the fragments created by the swollen iron should be put together; all the rest of the original fragments should be studied in order to identify the fragments which belonged to the same original block. This task was made more necessary by the fact that Balanos, in order to make a restorable architectural member, did not hesitate to put together fragments that did not belong together. To make them fit together he used to have the broken surfaces trimmed conveniently, a procedure that rendered our task even more difficult.

The fragments of the coffer ceilings restored by Balanos, were examined together with another 900 fragments which had been identified on the Acropolis rock. The results were spectacular: the fragments of the east portico slabs produced 26 groups of joining authentic fragments; the fragments of the west hall produced 216 groups of the same kind. Among the fragments of the west hall coffer slabs we made an important discovery: some of the slabs had four coffers instead of the usual two, which is the normal case (**Fig. 5**).The investigation of the beam fragments produced 11 groups of authentic joining fragments.

Another important task was the identification of the surviving fragments of six original Ionic capitals of the Propylaea in six groups of adjoining fragments. At the same time I produced drawings restoring the original form of the capital to full scale; these drawings proved indispensable for the accurate reproduction of two new Ionic capitals which were required for the new restoration (**Figs 8 a–c, 15–17 a–b**).

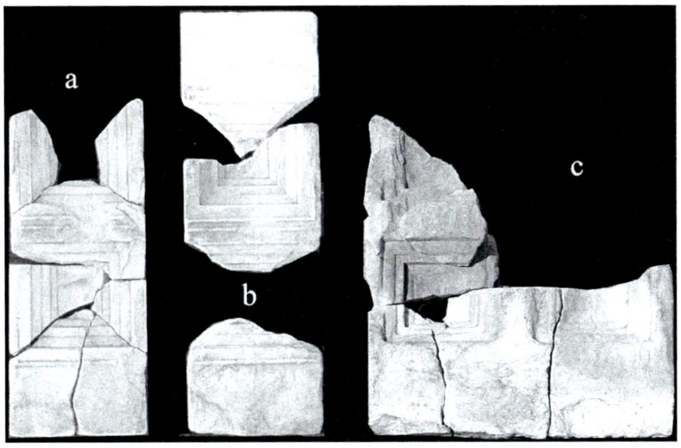

Figure 5 a-b: Two groups of adjoining fragments from the western hall ceilings (photo G. Vidos); **c:** A group of adjoining fragments belonging to a slab with four coffers

Figure 6 The south wall before, during and after the recent intervention (1997–2001)

In spite of the fact that the appearance of rusty iron elements was more evident in the north end of the east portico, the Acropolis Committee decided to advance with the dismantlement of the south end of the east portico, which had been shifted to the south and east by a gunpowder explosion in the past. The aim was to check the existence of Balanos' rusty iron clamps and dowels and to eliminate the deformation of the wall (**Fig. 6**).

This work started in 1997 and involved the dis-assembly and reassembly of 38 blocks. Important evidence on the original building techniques used in this edifice as well as its structural behaviour came to light. In particular, the extremely high quality of the Classical iron joints used, as well as the perfection of the lead sheathing, were revealed. Where the lead of the clamps was intact, the iron clamps had remained in perfect condition without any rusting (**Fig. 11a**).

The shifting of the wall towards the south and east distorted the double-T clamps that join the blocks horizontally. The clamps were stretched or broken in the middle lengthwise, that is in their deliberately weakest point. The danger of fractures in the marble was thus kept at bay; the great fractures in some of the blocks were caused by their geometric distortion as well as to the great mechanical stresses due to the modified static system of the entire structure.

The discovery of the inscription ΑΘΕ on some of the double-T clamps and dowels is highly important from an archaeological point of view, since no other examples of inscriptions on clamps and dowels are known. This inscription could be restored as ΑΘΕ (ΝΑΙΑΣ), or ΑΘΕ (ΝΑΙΩΝ) (**Fig. 7a-b**).

Many horizontal surfaces of the blocks were eroded in various points due to the opening of joints in the distorted wall. To recover the original cohesion, thin sheets of lead were inserted in the horizontal joints as the blocks were being reassembled. Thus, the final height of the wall was made equal to the original one. The vertical joints were never cemented, in order to avoid trapping water or other sources of energy inside the wall; only in one case where the joint had opened a few millimetres, the gap was filled with lead in order to prevent the blocks from coming closer in case of an earthquake. The work at the south wall of the east portico was completed in 2001.

After the dismantling in 1990–93 of the two coffer ceiling portions of the east portico and of the west hall, 107 more blocks from the previous restoration were still on the monument. The opinion of the Central Archaeological Board of the Ministry of Culture in favour of dismantling this last part as well, and of the restoration proposals, came in February of 2001 (**Fig. 8a-c**). The restoration proposals envisaged the use of the large number of newly-identified authentic fragments for the beams and the coffer slabs. The aim was to display the ceilings, which have always been the most admired feature of the architecture of the Propylaea, to best effect. The great

Figures 7a-b An iron dowel from the south wall of the east portico, bearing the inscription ΑΘΕ

a

b

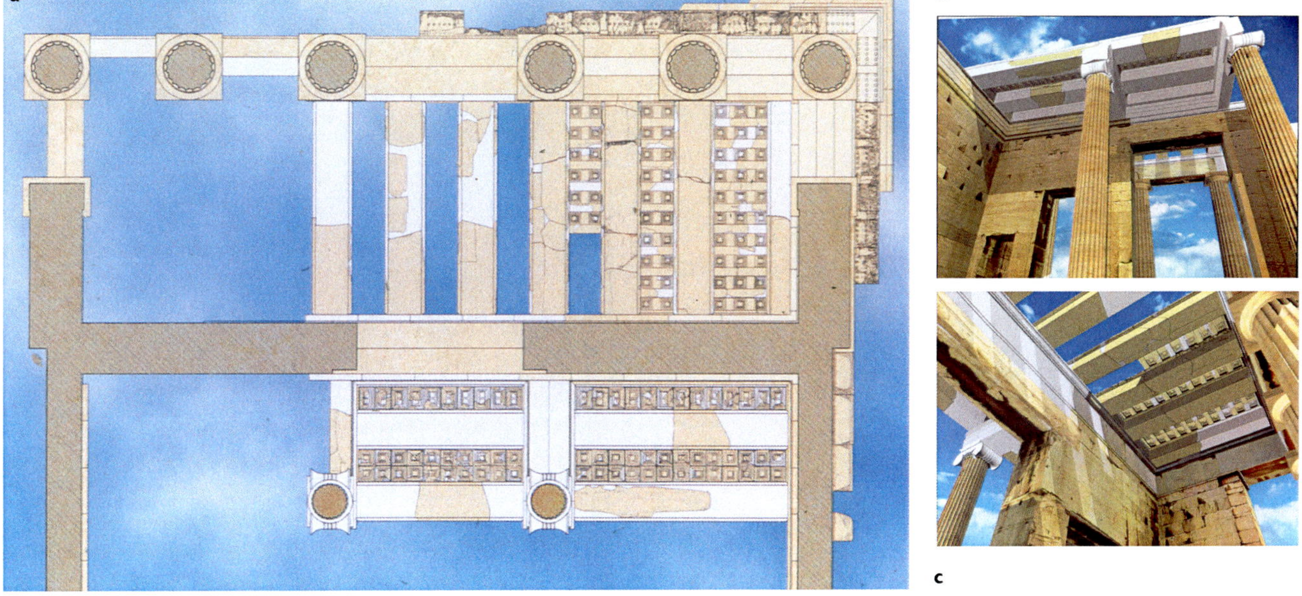

c

Figures 8a-c The restoration of the superstructure of the central building proposed in 2000. **a**: View from below; **b**: Perspective view in the western hall, from the west; **c**: Perspective view in the eastern portico, from the south (photo-realistic rendering by Th. Moutopoulos)

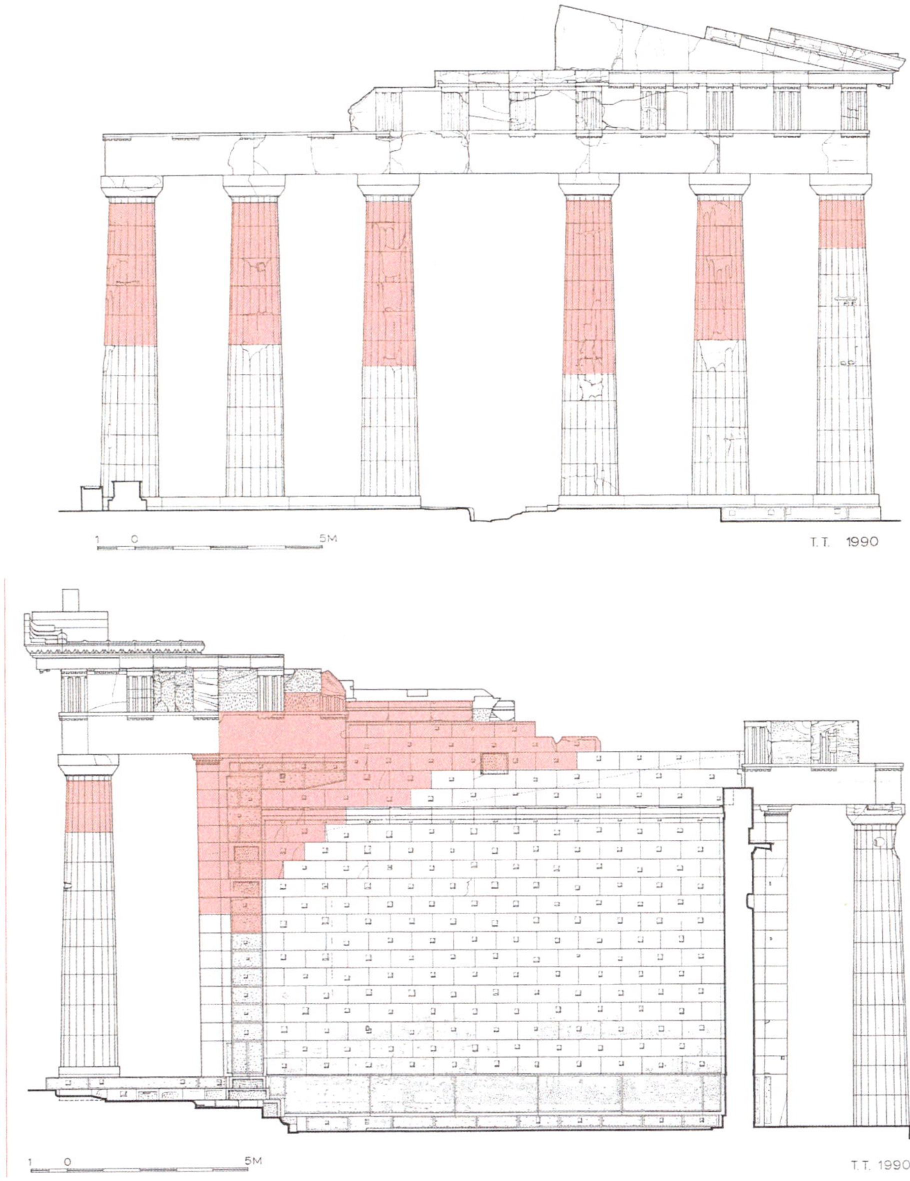

Figures 9a-b The east front and the north side of the central building. Pink indicates the blocks removed and restored by Balanos without an official report

Figure 10 The east portico after the completion of the dismantlement of the blocks restored between 1909–17 and before the beginning of the reassembly (May 2003)

number of coffer slabs provided the possibility of extending the restored ceilings above the central passageway, allowing visitors a proper sense of being inside the monument.

Dismantling began on 15 February 2002 with blocks of the pediment. It was soon noted that Balanos had modified the ancient system of construction during re-assembly. After the architrave blocks had been placed above the capitals, the superimposed blocks were 'built in'. To connect them, Balanos used brick, stone and marble fragments bound with mud, cement or lime mortar in addition to the clamps and various iron joints covered with lead or cement, as if it were a common wall. The blocks had thereby lost their independence which is one of the main characteristics of the original structure. Retaining this characteristic for every architectural component of the ancient structure has been one of the basic principles underlying the present anastylosis.

Once the 107 blocks of the superstructure of the central building were dismantled as planned, it became apparent that Balanos had dismantled and put back 43 north wall blocks and 24 column drums, without ever reporting this intervention (**Fig. 9a-b**). This discovery augmented the anticipated work to a large extent because, due to the advanced state of rusting in most of the metal joints used by Balanos, we were obliged to dismantle these blocks and column drums as well. In a few cases, blocks in situ were discovered to be in a rather poor condition. Their removal was deemed necessary so that their conservation could be performed in the laboratory. When the dis-assembly work ended in May 2003, instead of the anticipated 107 blocks, we had dismantled 192 blocks (**Fig. 10**).

During the work on the north wall of the central building, ancient double-T clamps were discovered, which had not been replaced by Balanos. Their original lead sheathing was not as carefully executed as the sheathing found on the south wall clamps. Furthermore, the iron of the clamps and dowels was clearly of inferior quality, since many of the extracted ones were in an advanced state of corrosion, although their lead sheathing had not been disturbed. Some bore the inscription ΑΘΕ, which had already been found in clamps and dowels in the south wall. There could be no doubt that the iron clamps and dowels of the northern wall are also Classical (**Fig.11b**). The poor quality of the iron and lead sheathing in the north wall, contrasted with the high quality of the same elements in the south wall, must be explained by the constraints imposed upon the architect after 434 BC by the Athenian administration combined with a shortage of fine Laconian iron ores, which was caused by the aggravated relations between Athens and Sparta. A study of the cuttings for dowels on the top surface of the two blocks of the central lintel make it clear that the superimposed course was laid starting from the south and north walls; in the middle, seven blocks were placed only after a considerable period of time had elapsed, as the technology of positioning and sheathing those dowels proves. This means that on the eve of the outbreak of the Peloponnesian war the superstructure of the Propylaea's central building was left incomplete (**Fig. 12a-c**).

On the upper surfaces of most of the column drums, inscriptions were found consisting of one letter of the alphabet (indicating the column) followed by parallel lines (indicating the position of the column drum). The letters indicating the columns of the east colonnade are (from north to south): Ε, Θ, Κ, Φ, Χ, Λ (**Fig. 13a**). The fine craftsmanship of the marble and the ingenuity of ancient builders are to be admired in these

a

b

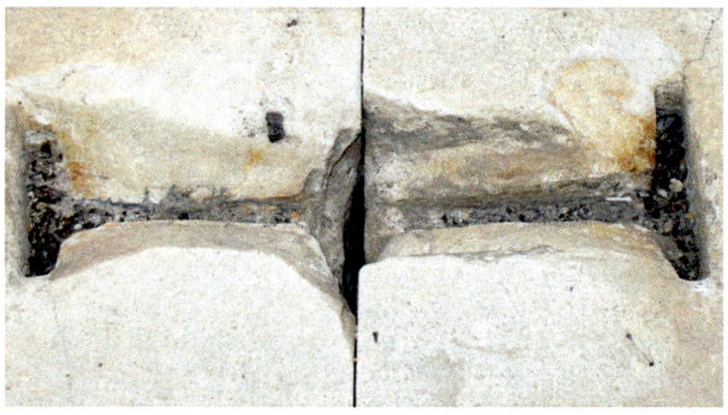

Figure 11a: A high quality classical clamp from the south wall, preserved in entirety; **11b**: A classical clamp from the northern wall almost totally disintegrated

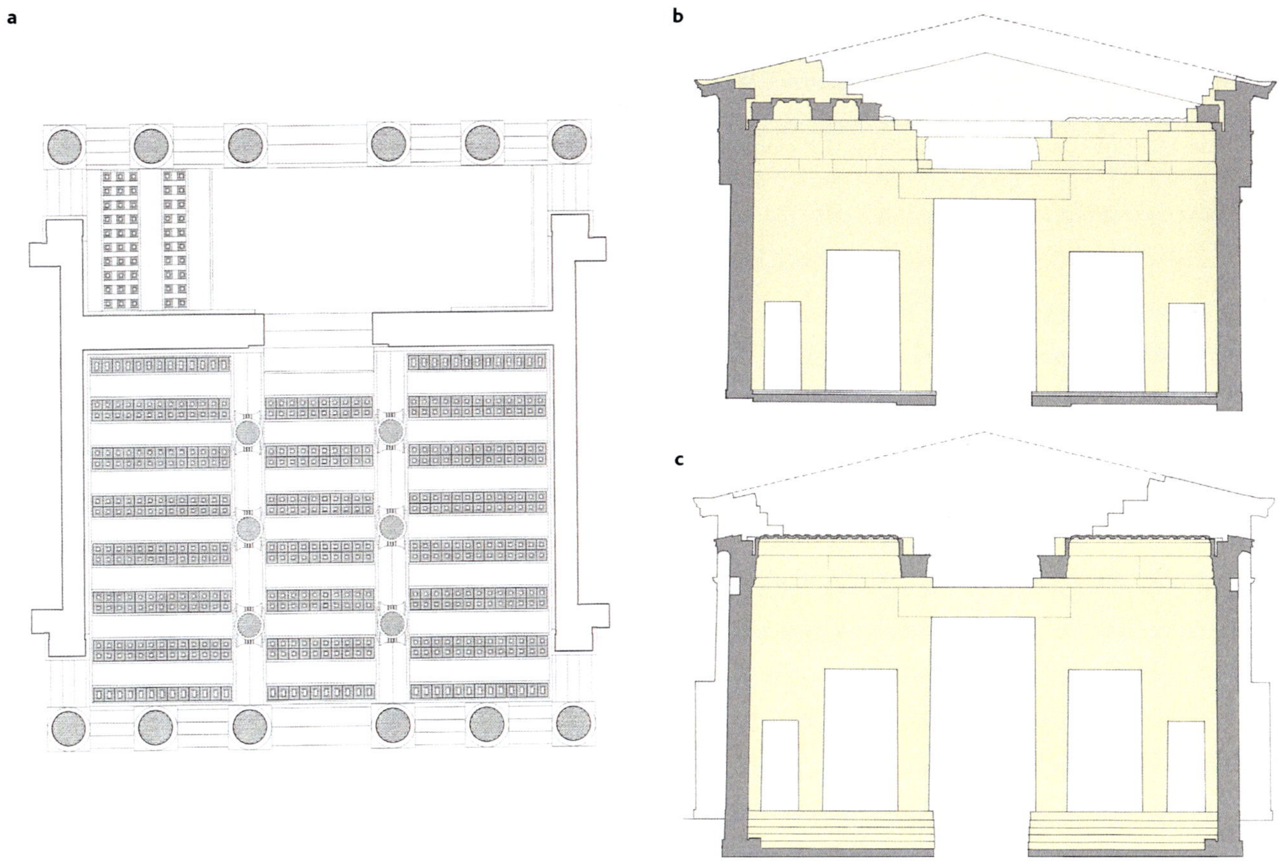

Figures 12a-c Parts of the Propylaea's central building superstructure that could have been built before the completion of the gap in the 18th course above the central lintel. **a**: View of the ceilings from below; **b**: Cross-section of the Propylaea's central building, facing the east side of the door-wall; **c**: Cross-section in the Propylaea's central building facing the west side of the door-wall

invisible parts of architectural members, and also in the manner in which damage – which took place during construction – was repaired **(Fig. 13b)**.

Re-assembly of the north wall blocks and drums of the east portico columns began in May 2003. Reproducing the structural characteristics of the original Classical structure is one of the most important principles to which the ongoing restoration of the Acropolis monuments aspires. The main bonding element is gravity through the friction developed between the horizontal surfaces of the blocks. In such buildings the architectural blocks are structurally individual, with sides properly shaped to provide sound contact with the neighbouring blocks. Before being restored back to their positions in the monument, each of the ancient blocks, or each group of fragments from an original block, is treated in ways that provide the necessary structural qualities, such as proper contact with the neighbouring blocks and sockets for the installation of clamps and dowels. This means first putting together fragments which come from the same original block, with the use of titanium rods and cement. New marble is added where it is necessary for the acquisition of the above qualities **(Fig. 14)**.

The restored blocks are put in their places without any mortar, with the addition of clamps and dowels made of titanium, sheathed in cement. It was very important for us to make each of the restored horizontal courses work as one solid course. For this reason, when it was necessary to leave a gap in the middle of a course, we filled it with lead.

Figure 13a: Classical inscription on the upper surface of the fourth column drum of the fourth column, counting from the north. In the central hole, remains of the empolion; **13b**: A piece of marble inserted in the upper part of a column drum for the repair of an arris damaged during original classical carving

In the entablature we used the new blocks inserted in the restoration by Balanos. We used new marble to fill the gaps created after the removal of ancient pieces improperly restored by Balanos. But for the huge beams of the ceilings (they are 6.4m long and weigh about 11 tons) Balanos had used almost exclusively ancient fragments. Because, in most cases, these did not belong together, we had to add new marble to the groups of original fragments which did not make up complete blocks.

We always restore to each ancient block its individual structural character, giving to it the dimensions it had in the original Mnesiclean structure. This is not always possible with the blocks made by Balanos because, as already mentioned, Balanos did not conceive his restoration as an absolute reproduction of the original building and structure, but as an approximation of the original forms, not caring for the exact dimensions and structural individuality of each architectural member. Also, he did not hesitate to have the Classical blocks trimmed in order to conform to the incorrect dimensions of his new architectural members. We always try to correct these discrepancies not at the expense of the authentic material, but at the expense of Balanos' or of the added material. This, of course, adds much work on the spot.

As noted earlier, the Classical iron double-T-clamps were constructed to be weaker in the middle so that, in the case of an earthquake, the clamp could be deformed and break, without causing the breakage of marble. In order to reproduce this refinement of the clamps, the long shaft of the double T titanium clamps are made thinner in the middle and the cement sheathing is interrupted in the middle of the shaft.

Figure 14 The fragments of an original ceiling beam are being put together by means of titanium bars and cement. General view and detail

Figure 15 Templates for the reproduction of the volutes of the new Ionic capitals. Templates were used for the exact translation of virtually every moulding of the originals into the new marble

Figure 16 Two views of one of the two modern replicas of Ionic capitals of the Propylaea. They are made in marble and sculpted by hand at the workshop of the Propylaea restoration project

In the carving of new marble elements, great care was given to the exact reproduction of the details of the Classical architectural forms. This was achieved by means of accurate measurements and templates. During this procedure it was realized once more that Balanos' architectural forms conformed only approximately with the Classical ones. Most demanding was the reconstruction of two Ionic capitals which were carved by hand. The original forms were restored according to existing fragments. The work took two very skilled men a total of 27 months. Thanks to the technical ingenuity of our marble technicians, the original design has been rendered with technical and artistic integrity worthy of that of the ancient originals (**Figs 15–16**). These capitals were restored on top of the easternmost columns of each of the Ionic colonnades framing the central passageway before the monumental central door of the door wall. The restoration in the west hall was completed in November 2008 and the scaffolding in this area was removed before the end of that year (**Fig. 17**). On 4 December 2009 the restoration of the eastern portico was completed and the scaffolding was removed by 19th of December 2009 (**Figs 17b, 18**).

The whole enterprise has involved the dismantlement, conservation and reassembly of 301 blocks and the incorporation in the structure of another 66 blocks and these latter blocks have been restored, for the first time, in the superstructure of the building above the central passageway. This allows the visitor to gain a sense of the proportions of the two roofed spaces of the main building of the Propylaea. In the end 367 architectural members have been put up, each weighing between 0.5 and 10.5 tons.

Figure 17a-b Views in the central building after the completion of the restoration; **a**: west hall; **b**: east stoa

Figure 18 The east front of the central building after the completion of restoration 2009

Figure 19 The restoration of 19 blocks on top of the south wall of the west hall seen from the south

The completion of the major project described above gives us the possibility to proceed with the restoration of other parts of the Propylaea, architectural members of which have been identified during my long investigations about the Propylaea in the last 35 years. In the south wall of the central building 17 blocks from the four upper courses have been identified and will be restored to their original positions, with the addition of only four small supplements in new marble. Among the identified blocks is the thranos (or inner cornice) in the British Museum. Since the restoration of this block on the Propylaea does not seem feasible in the near future, an exact copy in new marble has already been made in order to be included in the restoration. For the structural needs of the restoration of the identified blocks, two missing wall blocks had to be reconstructed in new marble. On completion of this intervention, 19 blocks will have been added on top of the south wall; three courses will be almost complete, the fourth consisting of only one original cornice block (**Fig. 19**). Nevertheless, the presence of this cornice block will allow the visitors to perceive the total shape of the south wall which, at the moment, is three courses lower than the north one. From the inside, the balance between the north and the south walls will be immensely enhanced allowing the full appreciation of the harmonious proportions of the Ionic hall.

Another important project that has recently obtained the official approval from the Ministry of Culture is the restoration of 51 original blocks in the superstructure of the south wing of the Propylaea. These blocks were retrieved from the demolition of the so-called Frankish Tower in 1885 that had been erected on the south wing by the Acciaiuoli rulers of Athens in the first half of the 15th century. The material had been studied by Bohn, Dörpfeld, Wood and Dinsmoor but it was never properly published or documented. Between 1946 and 1960, Anastasios Orlandos restored the westernmost column, the two piers, the epistyles of the west front and part of the fourth epistyle from the east. By 1978, at the start of my investigation, the material had been dispersed and, lacking proper documentation, I needed to identify it again and arrange it in groups of fragments which belong together. The blocks discussed above allow the restoration of the south wing up to the cornice level; the new marble that will be incorporated represents only 11% of the future restoration, including a complete frieze block which is needed in the west front (**Fig. 20a-d**).

One of the most interesting features of the restoration will be the marble cover of the south niche between the central building and the south wing; the bottom of this cover was flat, but the upper surface was carved to look like two very long pan-tiles divided by an equally long cover-tile running east-west. The free corner next to the column of the central building had a corner antefix, while the west end of the central 'cover-tile' had the form of a regular antefix. This hybrid element functioned at the same time as roof and as ceiling and as reminiscence of an entablature. It remained unique in its boldly unconventional character (**Fig. 21a-b**).

This intervention will restore the most intriguing part of the Propylaea that, in spite of and because of its being built following a heavily mutilated plan, demanded from the architect, in this case Mnesicles, solutions that created one of the most original architectural inventions. The restoration of the south wing is expected to be completed in 2013.

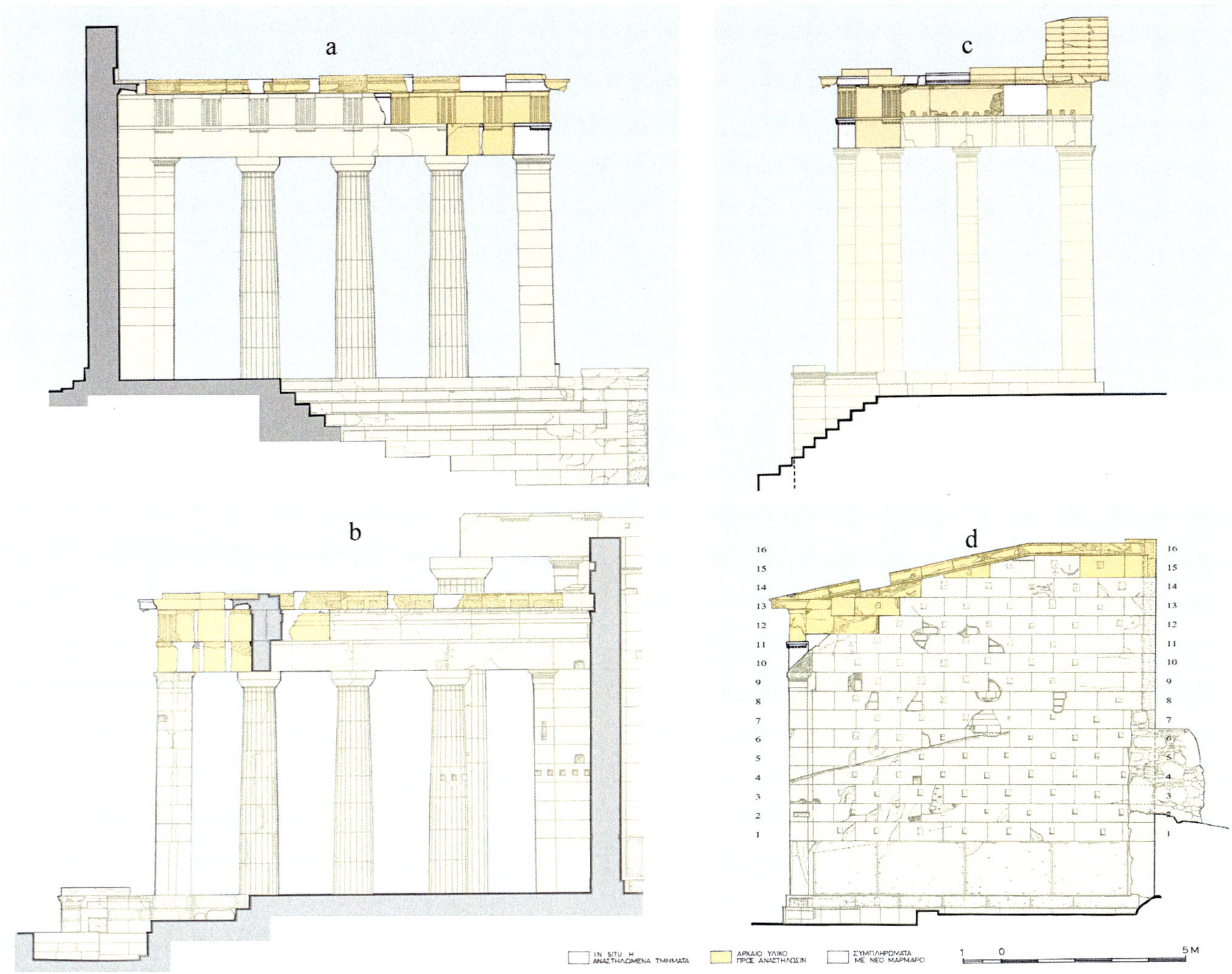

Figure 20a-d The south wing of the Propylaea after the restoration of the identified block in their original positions in the superstructure. **a,b**: Outer and inner views of the colonnade; **c**: The west front; **d**: Outer view of the south wall

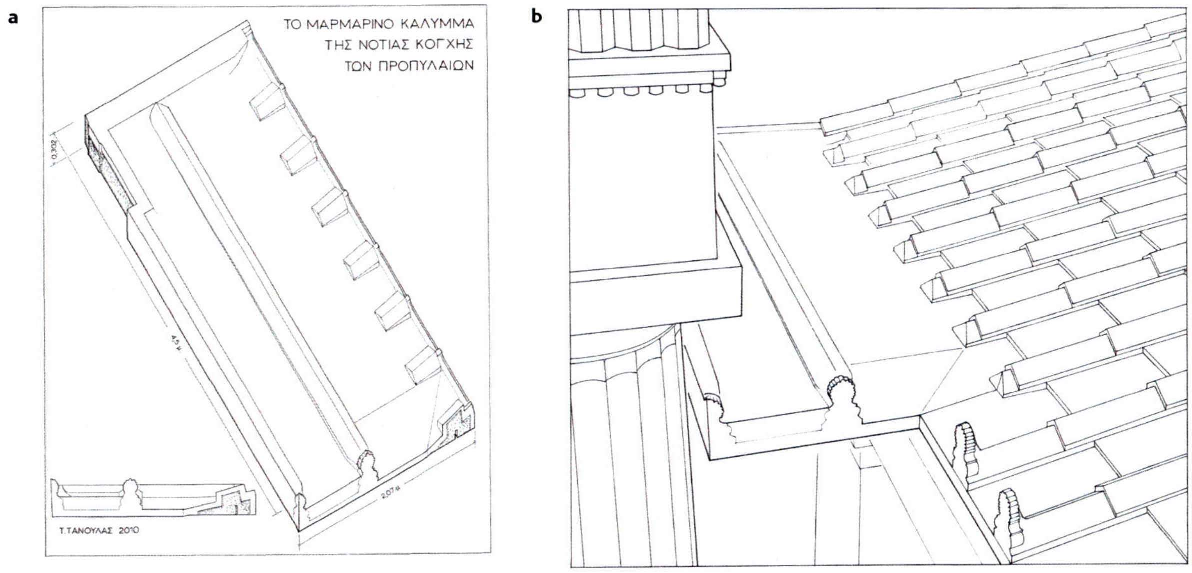

Figure 21a–b Marble cover of the southern niche. **a**: Aximetric view and west front. **b**: Perspective view from the north-west

The Temple of Athena Nike

Dionysia Michalopoulou

The temple of Athena Nike, designed by the architect Kallikrates, was built between the years 427 and 424 BC on the Classical bastion, south-west of the Propylaea of the Acropolis (**Figs 1, 2**). Built in the Ionic order, tetrastyle amphiprostyle, it replaced an earlier poros shrine, also dedicated to Athena Nike, which was discovered in 1936 beneath the Classical temple and on top of the Mycenaean bastion of the Bronze Age fortification.

The poros shrine lies at a depth of 1.8m below the level of the marble floor of the later temple. According to the epigraphic evidence (*IG* I² 24, *IG* I³), this is the earliest stone temple dedicated to the worship of Athena Nike. The sanctuary comprises a small poros temple Π-shaped in plan, which housed the *xoanon* of the goddess with its altar (**Fig. 3**).

The Classical temple and the bastion on which it is founded, in the form in which it is preserved today, is the product of a wider *anastelosis*, intended to restore the Classical monuments of the Acropolis.

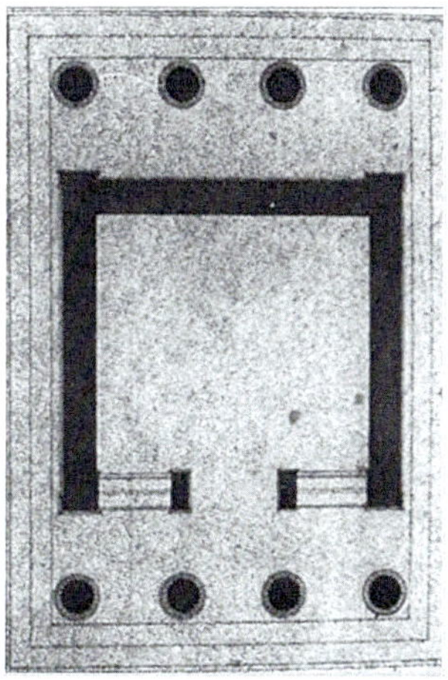

Figure 2 Plan of Athena Nike temple. (Drawing: H. Hansen)

Figure 1 The Temple of Athena Nike east and south facades after recent restoration. View from the south-east

Figure 3 The first stone shrine of Athena Nike within the Classical bastion

Figure 4 The temple of Athena Nike after the first restoration in 1835. View from the east. (Photo: J. Robertson and F. Beato 1857)

Figure 5 The temple of Athena Nike after the second restoration by Balanos and Orlandos, completed in 1940

The first *anastelosis* of the Nike temple was initiated in 1835 by Ludwig Ross, and was completed in 1845 by Schaubert, Hansen and Kyriakos Pittakis (**Figs 4, 5**). The second *anastelosis* was started in 1936 by Nikolaos Balanos and completed in 1940 by Anastasios Orlandos.

Because of the obvious structural problems, both in the foundations and in its superstructure (**Fig. 6**), a third restoration of the monument began on 6 October 2000, in accordance with a study made by the architect Demosthenes Giraud.

Dismantling of the architectural members of the temple, down to the krepis and including the blocks of the second step on the south side, was performed using the bridgecrane that was installed in 1997 on the level of the temple to assist in dismantling the members of the frieze, cornice and *sima* (**Fig. 7**).

As all the members of the krepis had to be dismantled, it was necessary to replace the bridgecrane with a new hoist system. The reasons were, first, the northward spread of the crane's pylons had been set over the members that had to be restored and, second, it could not be used for setting the columns vertically on the north side because of the limited length of the pylons' reach on the east-west axis.

Figure 6 Structural damage to the Athena Nike Temple architrave

Figure 7 Dismantling the Athena Nike Temple with bridge crane on scaffold, 2001

Following this, a new bridgecrane on scaffolding was installed (**Fig. 8**).

In the course of dismantling the architectural members of the temple, it was discovered that all had been damaged, specifically during the previous *anastelosis* (**Fig. 9**).

Where the marble faces had survived, the interior space had been filled with the amount of cement needed to give the cella wall its thickness. The marble faces and the filling material, the cement, were held together by exterior joining elements, such as Π-shaped clamps. The result of this was further cracking of the member because of the corrosion of the exterior clamps and their insufficient anchorage.

Damage was discovered in the members of the lower courses of the krepis because of rain. This resulted in the loss of a significant amount of the mass of their lower bedding surfaces as well as the cutting that resulted from deformations in the geometry of the temple and the setting of members in the wrong places. The trimming of the members was done during

Figure 8 The new bridge crane on scaffolding prior to the recent retoration

Figure 9 Damage to the members caused by the previous anastelosis, completed in 1940

Figure 10 The south facade of the temple of Athena Nike after the first anastelosis in 1835

the first partial *anastelosis* of the temple by Ross in 1835 (**Fig. 10**). Ross undertook *anastelosis* of the temple after it had been demolished by the Turks on the eve of Morosini's invasion in 1687. The members discovered by Ross built into a bastion west of the Propylaea, were set again in the krepis of the temple, which was intact but deformed by settling.

The damage found in members included perforations, cracks and extensive fractures, as a result of the differences in settling of the stones of the bastion, on which the temple is founded.

Members had broken and fragments belonging to them had disappeared (**Fig. 11**). To add fillings in order to restore the dimensions of the ancient members, the ancient surfaces were cut flat so that the fillings could be joined to them. The joining of the ancient with the new was accomplished with reinforcements, either exterior metal applied to the surface, or marble empolia.

Difficulties emerged in dismantling the blocks of the base of the wall with the cymation moulding. One reason for this was their fragmentation, caused by the use of surface reinforcements. Another reason was the emplacement of two more iron elements, circular in section, apart from the dowels, for the full height of the member, and driven into the underlying members.

Figure 11 The west facade of the temple of Athena Nike after the first anastelosis in 1835

Figure 12 Floor slabs revealed during the dismantling of the Balanos interventions

Figure 14 Concrete foundation of the Balanos interventions

During the dismantling six slabs made of new marble were revealed, having been inserted during the previous *anastelosis*. They covered a corresponding surface of unreinforced concrete 17cm thick (**Fig. 12**). These slabs were 10cm thick, as opposed to the 27cm thickness of the rest of the ancient slabs. The first and second steps of the *krepis* were dismantled and the interior surface, with an area of 30m², was found to be surrounded by the blocks of the courses referred to above. These had been filled in with non-reinforced concrete 30cm thick. Its removal brought to light marble fragments that Balanos had incorporated in the filling material. Many of these fragments have been recognised and attributed to blocks of the *krepis*, which had been filled in with cement rather than new marble. Extensive use of cement mortar was discovered between architectural members, on both horizontal and vertical joints (**Fig. 13**).

Particularly time consuming and demanding were the removal of fillings, the cleaning of cement mortar from the joints, the removal of reinforcements and also, because of the incorporated marble fragments, the removal of concrete.

The dismantling of the wall blocks of the cella revealed problems in their positions, mainly inconsistencies in the location of the sockets for the ancient dowels. After this, it was necessary to check the accuracy of their positions and to make a study for rearranging the blocks. This was carried out by the architect of the project Kostas Mamaloungas, whose study revealed the system of ancient key-stones, the initial position of the stone blocks and the change in position of 19 blocks out of a total of 108.

In the course of rebuilding the monument, the slab of reinforced concrete beneath the temple cella was removed, using the crasher method, a non-disturbing hydraulic concrete crasher, for cutting the rusted support system at the north-east corner of the temple, consisting of two twin metal rods of double T form, as well as the compact metal column in the basement of the temple that supported the north anta.

After the removal of the slab beneath the cella and the cleaning of the upper surface of the orthostates of the north wall of the earlier poros naïskos, it was evident that the salts that had been observed on those blocks and had damaged the poros stone, came from the peculiar construction of the foundation in concrete by the previous restorer (**Fig. 14**). It was then decided to dismantle six blocks of the north wall of the naïskos and, in order to prevent further salts from forming on the poros stones, to remove a wall, triangular in shape, of non-reinforced concrete, that lay against the entire length and height of the north wall of the naïskos.

The restoration programme of the monument continued with a redesign of the bearing construction on which part of the temple would be founded (**Fig. 15**). The space to be covered was a surface that was polygonal in shape, measuring about 15 m². In consultation with the present author and Prof. K. Syrmakezis, it was decided that a bearing structure made up of metal parts was the best solution. This involved the construction of a stainless steel grid of 316 L grade, with massive H-section (doubleT) beams, 20cm and 35cm in height.

Figure 13 Vertical surface of block coated in cement of the Balanos-Orlandos interventions

Figure 15 The bearing construction on which the temple of Athena Nike is restored

Figure 16 Marble filling in a column

Stainless steel sheets were placed on top of the grid, and welded in the middle to the upper flange of the beams, so that the welding seams are invisible to the visitor to the basement area.

This solution prevents rainwater from seeping through the joints of the floor slabs of the temple to the poros shrine beneath. A new floor slab was set in place of the light-well built by Balanos in order to provide light and air to the basement area.

The construction of the metal grid was a specialist task. The material was imported from Germany in the form of sheets. Then, in a workshop specialising in metal construction, the sheets were cross-cut to form the sections and welded.

The beams are supported on non-reinforced concrete that is surrounded, on the one hand, by the blocks of the two *krepis* steps with the *euthynteria* and, on the other, by a little wall of reinforced concrete that has replaced a section of the bearing wall of Piraeus stone in the basement space, another Balanos construction.

The replacement of part of the bearing wall mentioned above was considered necessary since, in any possible compression of the poros stone, the deflection would be greater than that determined for the double beam of the grid, that supports the north wall of the cella. In such a circumstance the north-east parastade (flanking wall) of the temple, and the temple itself, would therefore suffer undesirable deformations. In the space formed in the north and north-east part of the

Figure 17 The newly restored temple of Athena Nike; view from the north

Figure 18 West side of the frieze restored in cement casts

Figure 19 North side of the cornice

poros naïskos and in the places cleared of the solid base of non-reinforced concrete, two vertical elements or supports were constructed of grade 316 L stainless steel. One of these was to hold up the north-east corner of the temple, and the other the first column from the north and the north-east block of the *euthynteria*.

During the restoration of the Classical temple, nine undamaged members made of new marble of the previous *anastelosis* were replaced to provide resistance to compression, as their courses were not accurately horizontal. Likewise, all the fillings that had been added to the ancient fractured joints were removed from the architectural members of the temple. These included ancient marble from pieces scattered on the Acropolis, other pieces which were dubious components of the temple and, again, mortar. Scattered fragments were filled in with new Pentelic marble from the Dionysos quarry and incorporated in the monument as well as two intact members from the 'scattered pieces'.

An example of the filling of a column is shown in **Figure 16**. The previous repair, using a drum, disturbed the monolithic form of the column. The new filling was carved to respect the character of the original member.

New additions were added only where they were needed to restore the structural independence of the members and the fragments were joined with titanium by specialist personnel using the blind riveting method.

The dismantling of the 319 architectural members and the damage they had incurred meant that a large number of joins of fragments that belonged together was possible. During restoration of the monument, the following additional requirements in the work emerged:

1. A new bridge crane (**Fig. 8**) was installed in order to complete the programme of restoring the monument. Because of the peculiarity of the monument's location, it needed to cover a much larger area of level surface and of height than the previous one. For its static efficiency, foundation work of reinforced concrete was needed at the base of the bastion;
2. Foundation works for the siting of the metal grid;
3. Restoration of the members of the poros shrine;
4. Replacement of the cracked poros lintel between the poros naïskos and the altars.

The recent restoration of the temple of Athena Nike, in comparison with the two previous *anasteloseis*, introduced changes that restored the monument's original architecture and geometry. The principle ones are:

- The horizontal surface of the *krepis* of the temple, which after 1936 had a 4.5cm lean toward the west, has been recovered and corrected so that all the previously altered optical refinements of the monument are restored.
- The columns were restored more precisely to their original positions and were set in accordance with later building traces preserved on their shafts, thus retrieving previously unknown building phases of the mediaeval period and the Turkish domination (**Fig. 17**).
- The geometry of the cella was restored and this was verified in practice after the two trial settings of the blocks of the cymatium decorated base and the architrave.
- The initial positions of all the ashlar blocks of the temple have been verified after trial settings for the full height of the cella, before their definitive resetting.
- The coffered ceiling blocks were rearranged, in accordance with the building composition of the wooden infrastructure of the roof of the temple.
- Copies of the frieze of the temple in cast cement were set in place on the monument (**Fig. 18**).
- The cornice, pediment and sima were restored in agreement with the greatest variation given in the architectural study (**Fig. 19**).
- The east view of the temple has been vastly improved, for its last missing part has been recovered: the pediment, with the addition of most significant authentic fragments, which for many years had lain scattered on the Acropolis.

The summer of 2010 saw the works of restoration of the temple of Athena Nike completed. Once again the monument commands the western approach to the Acropolis (**Figs 20–21**).

Figure 20 The Nike temple and bastion

Figure 21 The Nike temple from south-west

The Parthenon

Nikos Toganidis

The Parthenon (**Fig. 1**), that masterpiece of Classical art and architecture, was built on the Acropolis of Athens between the years 447 and 438 BC by the architects Iktinos and Kallikrates and the sculptor Pheidias, who took 5 more years to place the sculptures in position on the pediments. The temple was dedicated to the goddess of wisdom Athena and survives to this day. The main material of the construction was the famous white marble, excavated from Mt Penteli close to Athens (**Fig. 2**). The temple construction was financed by public money, mainly deriving from silver mines in Laurium (**Fig. 3**).

Historical phases and restorations

The solid rock of the Acropolis on which the Parthenon was built, and the material and the quality of its construction, are most probably the reasons why, in a country with so many earthquakes, the Parthenon has survived for about 2,500 years. The present state of the temple is a consequence of human actions of which the most significant are set out below.

1. A great fire occurred in the Roman period (AD 267) when a northern warrior tribe, the Heruli, invaded Athens and destroyed the city. They also burnt the Parthenon. The huge wooden beams of the roof naturally caught fire. The inferno lasted many days and destroyed among other elements most of the inner facade of the cella and, while burning the roof, damaged the back of the hexastyle colonnades of the short sides of the temple.
2. In the 6th century the Parthenon was converted into a Christian church. In the process, the eastern entrance was blocked while a semicircular apse was created by reusing and re-carving parts of the structure. Also, about 9–10 windows were opened on the long sides, by breaking marble members on those sidewalls and six blocks of the Ionic frieze were removed, three on each of the long sides.
3. In 1687 the Venetian forces besieged the Turkish garrison on the Acropolis. A bomb ignited the gunpowder which the Turks were storing inside the Parthenon at the time. The temple was split in two. Fourteen columns on both the north and south sides collapsed as well as part of the walls of the cella.
4. In 1802, Lord Elgin's workmen broke the edges of the surrounding marble while detaching and removing large sculptural elements on the temple. In order to lighten the

Figure 1 Parthenon from the south-east

Figure 2 Penteli Mountain. Marble quarry

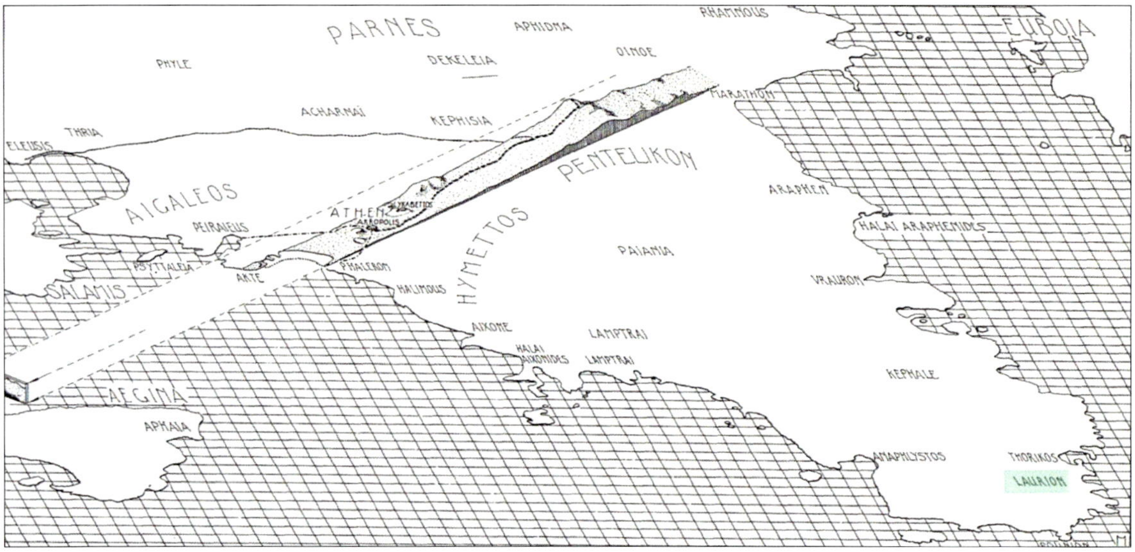

Figure 3 Plan of Attica. (Drawing: M. Korres)

load of the blocks of the frieze, saws were used to reduce their depth and cut away the sculptured surfaces. Eleven remnants from these mutilations have been found on the Acropolis. The Turks, after this damage was done, pulled down the major part of the walls.

5. The first effort at the restoration of the Parthenon by Kyriakos Pittakis in 1842–44 began after the liberation from the Turks. He partially restored the side walls of the cella and part of the north colonnade.
6. The second extensive restoration effort started in 1898–1902 and continued in 1922–33 by the civil engineer Nikolaos Balanos.
7. A violent earthquake that took place in 1981 affected the corners of the east side and obliged the authorities to take action, so in 1984 the third extensive restoration project started.

These then are the principal historical events that have affected the physical condition of the Parthenon. Let us now turn to the programme of restoration. Given its wide range and great scale, it was necessary to divide the work into 12 parts. A number of these parts are now complete.

- East elevation (completed, 210 members)
- East inner hexastyle colonnade (completed, 64 members)
- East wall (73 members)
- South wall (partial, 570 members)
- North wall (partial, 385 members)
- North elevation (completed 230 members)
- West wall (25 members)
- Partial roof of the west corridor (35 members)
- West inner hexastyle colonnade (completed)
- West elevation (78 members)
- South elevation (partial 112 members) partially restored
- Floor/steps (partial 36 members)

During the preparation of the restoration site in 1984, all marble members lying around the Parthenon on the Acropolis and some outside the Acropolis area were collected together. For the transportation of these marbles, owing to the uneven ground of the area, we used a flexible system of metal beams and metal tubes and a lifting machine, a kind of monorail, combined with a wheelbarrow.

Before the restoration project began, in order to protect the ancient marble floor, a concrete screed was laid down in the interior of the Parthenon cella. On this 'working' floor, a Derrick-type crane was installed. The installation of this crane was designed to be done by hand, due to the remoteness of the location.

First, we started dismantling the north-east corner. After the dismantling of the members above the corner columns (Fig.

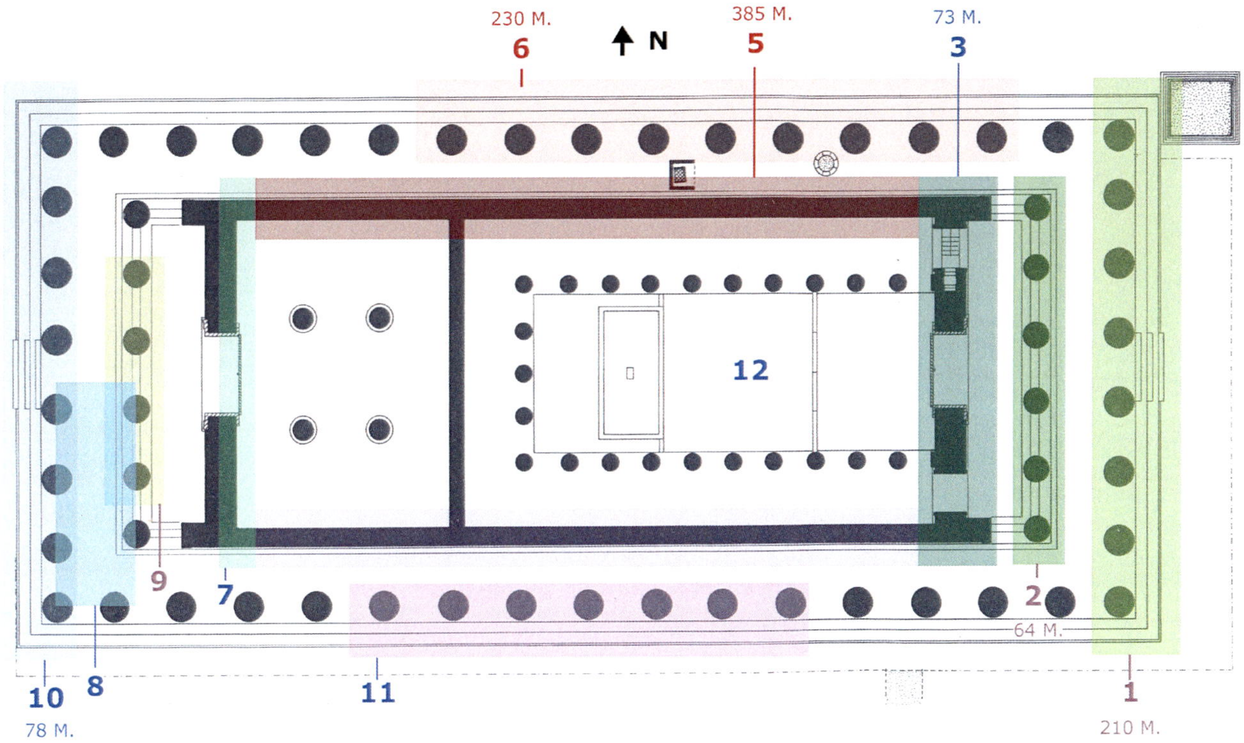

Figure 4 Parthenon: the restoration programmes

5), these columns were released from pressure, and so relaxed on their bases. We checked and made sure that their foundations were in good condition.

Owing to earthquakes, the south-east column and its capital had been rotated as one. As is well known, all of the exterior columns are inclined inwards for aesthetic reasons. It is clear that the corner column has very special geometric parameters. So, any rotation, affects the curvature of the architraves. Therefore, to correct this distortion, we designed a way to rotate the column back to its original position (**Fig. 7**). In order for the whole column to pivot, we tied a metal beam on the lowest drum and pushed it horizontally and, at the same time, we pushed the capital on the top, with a force oriented towards the selected rotation point. For safety reasons, we installed a system with brakes, to avoid rotation more than necessary (**Fig. 7**).

After we resolved this serious restoration problem, we continued replacing all of the original 'metopes' and statues, with copies made of a special concrete. We also rearranged some members, to their original position. Newly found ancient fragments were also incorporated into the pediment on this side.

In total more than 300 tons of marble were removed, conserved and their position rearranged. The next ambitious programme was the restoration of the east inner hexastyle colonnade (**Fig. 8**). The study proposed four choices, ranging from a minimum to a maximum degree of restoration. The inner faces of the columns were damaged by fire. So, a restoration without marble completions of these areas was not possible. This restoration affected the final appearance of the monument (**Fig. 9**).

On the south side, the fifth column was severely tilted outwards. So, we decided to carry out only a part of the programme, for considerations of safety that had to do with the monument's stability. This kind of column weighs 50 tons. It was therefore of great concern that 1/5th of the lowest drum of this column was entirely missing. Previous restorers had filled part of the drum's mass with stones and marbles, which did not really support the column. But this was not the only problem. Apart from the inclination of the column, there was a major rotation from the original position. The decision concerning the restoration was difficult, because the condition of the column above the first drum was perfect. Finally, we decided to treat the column as a whole, in order to repair the bottom drum.

This was achieved by means of a simple system. A concrete base was constructed around the column and extended inwards about 2m, with a height equal to the lowest drum. A metal construction was assembled around the second drum, in order to raise and transport the entire column by sliding it on metal plates. We then took off all members of the superstructure. The column was hung on the metal construction by common tension screws tied on the second drum.

Afterwards, we raised the entire column some millimetres from its base. Then, by using two huge screws and manpower provided by eight men, we pushed the entire column inwards, also forcing partial rotation from time to time. Then, we repaired the base, by completing the missing parts with new marble. At the time when the column was sliding backwards to its original place, we completed the necessary rotation by changing the position of the screws. This effort was completed successfully. And as far as we know, this approach to solve this kind of restoration problem is the first of its kind.

The restoration continued with the north and south long walls of the cella. That is to say parts four and five. The walls comprise 17 rows of stones of typical modular length mounted on orthostates. This configuration characterizes the Parthenon walls. All odd rows consist of full-width marble stones, 114cm thick and all in even rows, consisting of two stones per width, one on the exterior and the other on the interior face of the wall.

Figure 5 Dismantling the north-east corner

Figure 7 Rotation design of the south-east corner column. (Drawing: M. Korres)

Figure 6 Parthenon bird's eye view

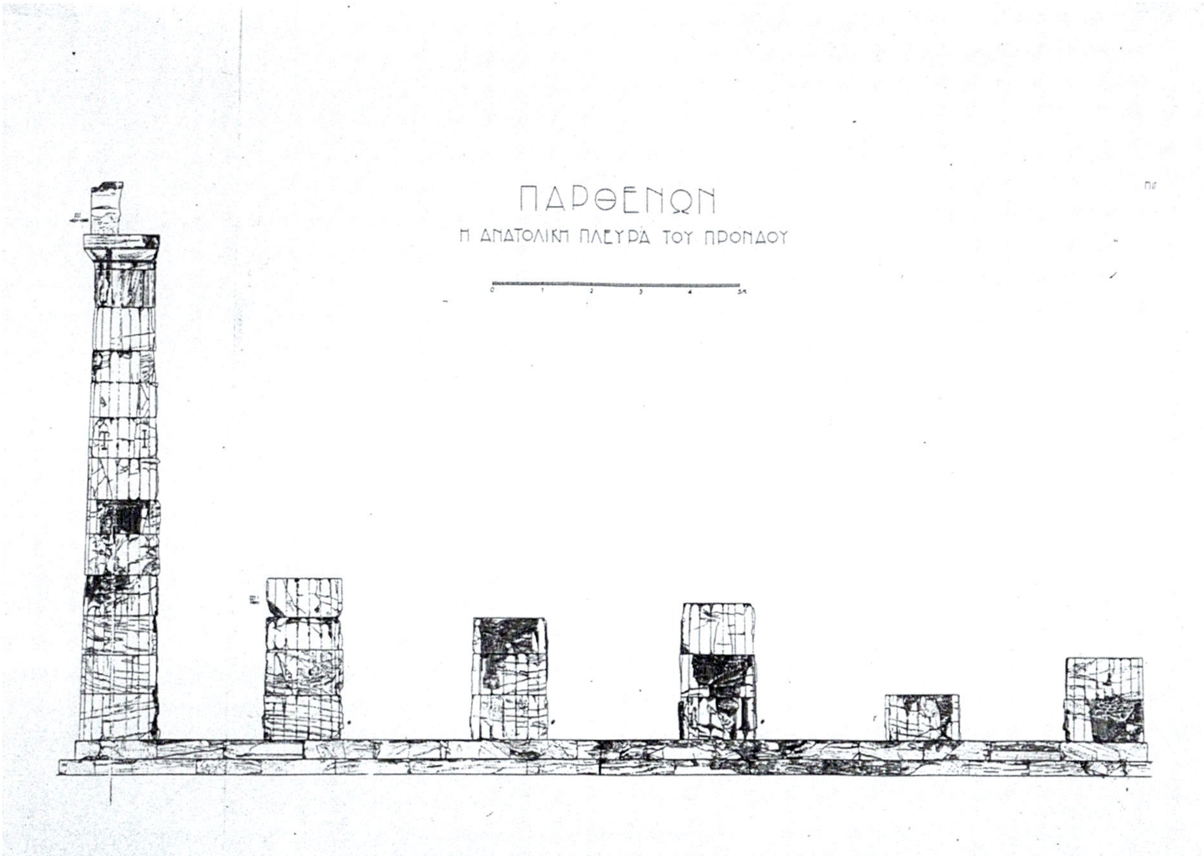

Figure 8 Pronaos before the restoration. (Drawing: M. Korres)

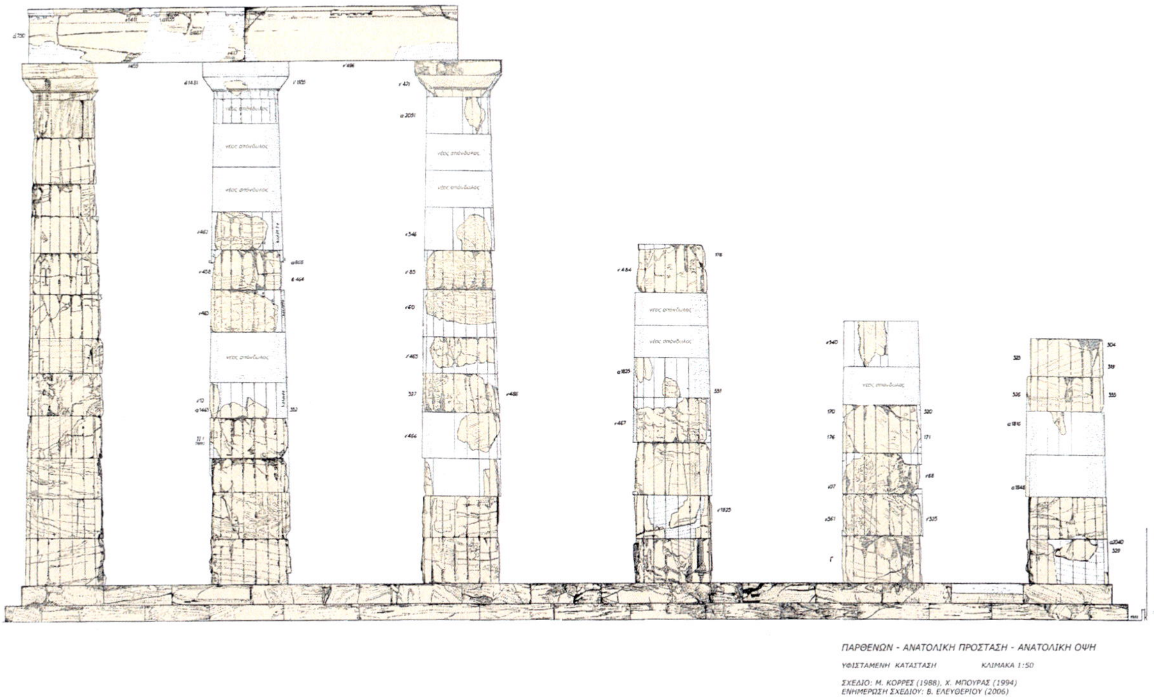

Figures 9 Pronaos after the restoration. (Drawing: M. Korres)

The fire which took place in AD 276 damaged the interior facade of the walls. An average depth of 25cm from their mass is lost forever. In addition, the explosion brought about the blocks' destruction, and especially fragmenting the sections which were connected by metal elements.

In 1992 we secured approval to dismantle the areas previously restored by Pittakis and Balanos in order to arrive at the ancient original design and take this as the new starting point for our study.

In this way, we gathered a total of 750 stones – the dismantled ones as well as those scattered on the ground. Our main target was to confirm their original position. We developed a lot of techniques in order to detect the answers. We spent about 10 years on this, while doing other projects at the same time on the Parthenon. And by re-evaluating our way of working, we moved towards a traditional technique as a solution. We processed this information through a computer programme, in order to manage the huge amount of data, we used common software tables. And so far, we have recognized the original position of 536 marble blocks belonging to the long walls. This means, more than 2/3 of the 750 blocks mentioned before have been allocated to their original position on the structure (**Fig. 10**).

This archaeological problem-solving was supplemented with a minimal amount of new marble to stabilise the structure. Today, this solution is to be taken further by civil engineers in collaboration with architects in order to achieve the best results aesthetically and structurally.

The next part was the restoration of the west inner hexastyle colonnade. A start was made by dismantling the area above the architraves and conserving the original members. Owing to our fears regarding the stability of the original columns that were seriously damaged in the fire, we stopped the dismantling. The idea was to increase the stability of the columns. We did not even consider dismantling the drums, because of their bad condition. So, we developed two special grouts, which were passed through the thin cracks of the burned marble. Two network systems of pipes were installed on each drum. Through the first network we squeezed the grout into the cracks, measuring both quantity and pressure. The second pipe network allowed the air to escape.

Having thus increased both the coherence and the stability of the columns, the next phase was to dismantle and conserve the rest of the members. Some of the inner architraves showed serious chemical metamorphosis on the ancient mass of marble, due to the effects of the fire.

The original sculpted members of the frieze were removed and sent to the laboratories of the old Acropolis Museum for conservation and cleaning. We put in their place substitutes made of an advanced concrete mixture, which were exact replicas of the originals in their position on the temple (**Figs 10–11**). Behind this replica, a new marble stone completed the original volume and supported the loads of the superstructure. A special anchoring system made of stainless steel, was used as a connection item between the two (**Fig. 11**).

The capitals, also, were found not to be in good condition. We also had to repair one column drum under a capital. However, we were lucky in the fact that we found its original wooden *polos* and *empolion* in a good condition. In this restoration we substituted wooden *poloi* and *empolia with* titanium ones (**Fig. 12**).

This phase of work finished in 2004 (**Fig. 13**). Since 2001, however, we had also undertaken the restoration of the north elevation (**Fig. 14**). This part, now complete, was the largest and most difficult so far. Most of the damage was due to the corroded iron from the previous restoration. In this phase, we restored the colonnades using Pentelic marble completions and replacing the concrete ones from Balanos' time. This intervention included an area of eight columns, out of a total of 17 in the north colonnade, which were affected by the explosion of gunpowder that blew down this area (**Fig. 15**). We had dismantled about 230 architectural blocks. In a few cases we dismantled more than was strictly necessary, in order to find out more information as to their original design. For example: in order to look for marks at the bottom of the column.

After restoring the drums and taking off the concrete completions, in some cases we discovered an incredibly bad situation hidden underneath. Structural elements, such as architraves, required the fixing of 26 fragments in order to regain a single architectural member.

Figure 10 Restoration of the west frieze

Figure 11 Restoration of the west frieze

Figure 12 Original empolion found inside the 5th west inner column

Figure 13 Opisthonaos; view from the north after the restoration

Figure 14 North side during dismantling

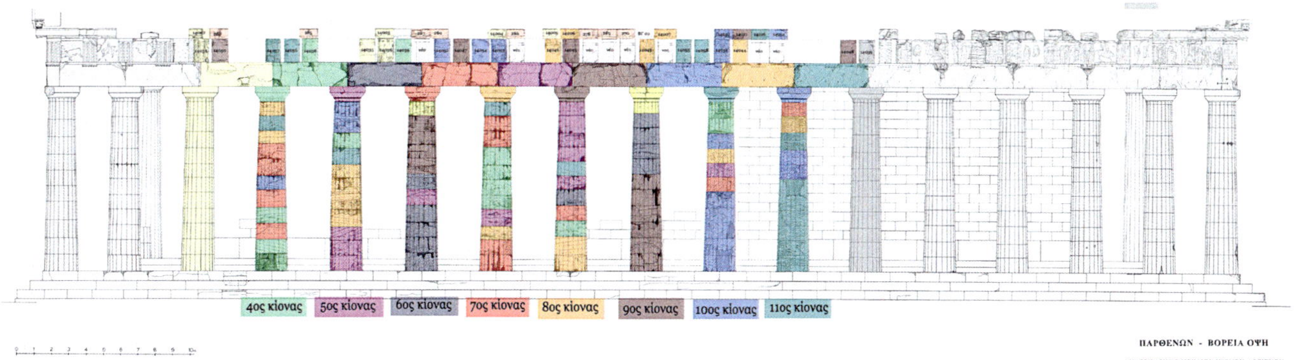

Figure 15 North elevation rearrangement of architectural members

Figure 16 Restoration works on the west end of the north entablature

Figure 17 Scattered fragments found their original position

Figure 18 West end of north side entablature

We rearranged the drums in order to obtain for each column an equal overall total height and normal *entasis*. Specific studies were first made with accurate measurements. At this point, all blocks of the superstructure were on the ground. We separated them from their preceding incorrect concrete completions, and we succeeded in finalizing the correct order of the superstructure blocks. The curvature of the architraves was therefore also restored (**Figs 16 and 17**).

The work on the north side was extended to the west end (**Fig. 18**), in order to remove the original metopes and send them to the Museum for conservation and cleaning. This part of the restoration lasted until June 2009. Today carvers are giving the final touches to the new drum completions.

The next part of the programme will be the west side, because serious structural damage remains. There is an approved study and we are organizing the rearrangement of the equipment on the site. The crane will move from the north to a new base in front of the west colonnade.

From the first to last part of the programme, about 1,900 architectural members in total will have been removed and restored.

The challenge of this work required all those involved from marble carver to engineer to excel beyond what had seemed humanly possible. We set our standards at levels that not only show respect for the beauty and supreme craftsmanship of the monument, but also for the ancient masters who made it.

The Parthenon North Side

Lena Lambrinou

The north colonnade of the Parthenon closely reflects the turbulent history of the monument as a whole (**Fig. 1**). The destruction of the building in 1687 during bombardment by Venetian troops under General Morosini abruptly ushered in a new phase in the monument's history as a famous ruin (**Fig. 2**). During this destruction, the central sections of the long colonnades on the north and south sides of the building collapsed along with the long walls of the cella and the roof. The north colonnade of the building lost its eight central columns and their entablature, which collapsed in a huge pile of rubble. As a ruin, over the next two centuries, the Parthenon was used as a source of building material and of sculptures for sale.

With the foundation of the modern Greek state in the third decade of the 19th century, the spiritual revival of the Greek nation came to be seen as interconnected with the survival of the ancestral relics. The quest for the picturesque, '...that kind of beauty which looks well in a picture', as it was defined by William Gilpin in 1782 (**Fig. 3**) and the fascination among Europeans for Greek antiquities, particularly those of the Classical period in the 5th century BC, influenced the attitude of specialists and the public towards the architectural and sculptural remains of other periods. This Classical centrism cultivated in the consciousness of modern Greeks the idea of an unbroken continuity with the golden age of Periclean Athens and encouraged a selective attitude among Greek authorities regarding which antiquities to save.

The question of 'Which Parthenon should we save?', was an ideological issue posed at the first International Congress of Archaeologists in Athens in 1905 and was one which had tormented intellectuals through the 19th and 20th centuries. It had already been practically resolved quite effortlessly in the 1830s by the Neoclassical Bavarian architects who worked for Greece's first king, Otto, and who played a decisive role in the preservation of ancient Greek monuments. The purism that marked the adoration of Greece's Classical past most prominently pursued on the Athenian Acropolis greatly influenced efforts to clear away medieval and even Roman remains in 19th century Greece in the name of preservation of antiquities.

Figure 1 The Parthenon in the 17th century, by H. Omont. (Reproduced by kind permission of the Gennadius Library, American School of Classical Studies at Athens)

Such purist ideological orientation led to an essentially stylistic restoration of the Parthenon, in accordance with the pattern of early 19th-century France and the 'Roman principles' of Italy where the idea of preserving the remains of antiquity to glorify their current owners first crystallized. Ruinous ancient buildings were seen as works of art, with every disfigurement to their form being accepted and preserved with respect for their original material, as was established in the 17th century by antiquarian Bellori and in the 18th century by the great Johann Joachim Winckelmann. This approach contributed to a theoretical emphasis on the material authenticity of monuments and as the Conseil des Batiments recommended in France in 1807 the need to preserve monuments in the condition in which they were found without any changes, aside from those needed to strengthen their structure and provide greatest durability over time. Later, in 1832, the architect Quatremère de Quincy emphasised the need to preserve ruins with an educational aim and advocated the filling-in of missing sections in a simplified way, as J. Jokilehto mentions.

The amalgamation of these ideas of material authenticity and didactic in-filling paved the way for the restoration ideology applied to the Acropolis monuments by well-known personalities of the era, including the archaeologist Ludwig Ross, the architect Christian Hansen and, above all, the talented Leo von Klenze. Klenze, advisor to King Otto's father, came to Greece in 1834 to redraw Athens' city plan. He stayed for only three months, yet influenced more than anyone else the interventions on the Acropolis. Upon departing, he left behind a detailed programme for the works, a budget, and even a list of architects to be responsible for the restorations.

During this period of the 1830s the term anastelosis (the putting of fallen members back on a building) had not yet been coined. It was only introduced a century later. Instead, interventions were described by A. Rangavis in 1837, as either a '... new erection' of the monuments, a '...renovation...', or '...the erection or completion of the antiquities...'. It was also said that the monuments '...should be erected in their ancient position and form...'. Other voices opposing all such interventions which came primarily from British commentators arguing that they would destroy the historicity of the ruins and from antiquarian circles and intellectuals such as William Mure were not heeded. They proposed a romantic approach to the monument, foreshadowing the anti-Restoration movement, which was not compatible with the neoclassical spirit of the Bavarian court and its need to manage properly ancient monuments such as the Parthenon for the glory of their King.

The first interventions on the Parthenon in the 1830s were characterized by great optimism, but impoverished means. They started within a climate of euphoria and national pride, and according to von Klenze's guidelines from the Parthenon's north colonnade. The north side, as von Klenze noted, 'is that which can be seen from the city and (primarily) from the palace that is, from the most important sides' and should thus be erected first. Aesthetics were clearly the main factor in planning the intervention, which promoted a stylistic restoration through the clearing and removal of medieval remains. The area was also stripped of all activities except for archaeology with the removal of dwellings and the prohibition of military use of what had until then been a fortress.

The launch of the Acropolis interventions was characteristic of the romantic spirit of the day: on 10 September 1834, Leo von Klenze organised a festival, presided over by King Otto, to celebrate the start of the *anastelosis* on the Acropolis and especially on the Parthenon. The king was to be seated on a wreathed throne in the middle of the temple's cella. For this occasion, Otto was symbolically to set one of the column drums of the north colonnade.

In this first decade of the Acropolis interventions, technical and economic difficulties prevented much of what von Klenze had proposed for the Parthenon from being completed. A heavy

Figure 2 The Parthenon in 1749 after the destruction of 1687 by a Venetian bombardment, by R. Dalton. (Reproduced by kind permission of the Gennadius Library, American School of Classical Studies at Athens)

Figure 3 The Parthenon in 1834 prior to any restoration, by C. Hansen. (Reproduced by kind permission of the Royal Library, Copenhagen)

lifting machine, designed by von Klenze and ordered in 1835, finally arrived on the Acropolis in 1841. This machine was able to raise the fallen column drums, capitals and architraves of the north colonnade, each of which weighed 8 to 9 tons. The intervention finally began in 1842 after the Bavarians stepped down and the powerful, but amateur archaeologist Kyriakos Pittakis Ephor of the Ministry of Education's Archaeological Service, took charge of the operation. Supported by funding from the Archaeological Society of Athens, Pittakis started with the partial restoration of the Parthenon's ruined north colonnade.

The amateur Pittakis followed von Klenze's directions faithfully. Identification of sections of the north colonnade lying on the ground was easy since, after the 1687 explosion, almost all of its architectural members were lying to the north of the Parthenon. Pittakis, in collaboration with the archaeologist Alexandros Rizos-Rangavis, was limited to the full reconstruction of only two columns and the partial restoration of four others. In total, he reset 30 drums and two column capitals (**Fig. 4**).

Pittakis' empirical intervention, assisted to some degree by Rangavis, was not based on any systematic study or documentation of the building and was described as '... unmethodical and by chance ...' even by the collaborator Rangavis himself. Pittakis reset column drums randomly, without regard for their original positions the only criterion perhaps having been their state of preservation. Missing parts of the columns were filled with brickwork in a simple cylindrical form without following the shape of the fluting. The brickwork, consisting of machine-made bricks was similar to

Figure 4 The north colonnade of the Parthenon after Pittakis' restoration in 1846, by A. Paccard. (Reproduced by kind permission of the Ecole Nationale Supérieure des Beaux-Arts)

Figure 5 Temple of Ceres at Paestum after the interventions of 1828. (Photo: the author)

the method used in contemporary Italian interventions on ancient Greek temples such as that on the Temple of Ceres at Paestum by Antonio Bonucci in 1828 (**Fig. 5**). The implementation of this Italian method was necessitated by construction needs and may have been the cheapest way to fill the lacunae on the members. Adapting marble additions to the missing drum parts, and carving flutes on such marble fillings, would have been a much more difficult, expensive process, due to the scarcity of skilled marble masons in Greece at this time. Pittakis' idea was to complete the north colonnade, but financial difficulties forced him to terminate the project in 1844 before its completion. Afterwards, the negative assessment of this first *anastelosis* on the Parthenon, the criticism of Pittakis' amateurism and the lack of a scientific approach and technical expertise led to a significant change in the choice of restorers for the next phase of interventions.

The Balanos intervention

Half a century after Pittakis a new era began in the late 19th century with the interventions of Nikolaos Balanos a civil engineer trained at the National School of Bridges and Roads (École Nationale des Ponts et Chaussées [ENPC]) in Paris. His intervention was distinguished by its invasive methodology. Archaeologists had given way to engineers, who were trained in construction, but who lacked any kind of archaeological education. The employment of Greek engineers and technicians established a new scientific standard for the structural and static strength of the ensuing 20th-century interventions.

Characteristic of Balanos' intervention on the north side of the Parthenon was the dynamic resolution of static problems and the use of methods derived from contemporary construction techniques which, however, were previously untested on ancient monuments. Balanos attempted better to resolve the Parthenon's aesthetic problems resulting from the initial restoration and fulfilled the vision of the earlier restorers regarding the completion of the north colonnade.

This approach to the monument from a purely constructional perspective may indeed have resolved the complex problem of the static durability of the restored, heavy members, but it also demonstrated an astonishing ignorance of the new materials to be used. In particular, in using reinforced concrete, Balanos seems to have misunderstood its material qualities and, consequently, to have overestimated its resistance to moisture and weathering. Although the reinforced concrete employed in filling in the Parthenon's column drums was selected with a strong conviction that casing the iron clamps with cement was a sufficient measure to protect them against rust, Balanos did not acknowledge the porosity of the cement itself. It is indeed surprising that the 'Committee for the Conservation of the Parthenon', of the Ministry of Education, which then approved the initial proposals, and Balanos himself remained impassive to the warning bells sounded by Joseph Durm as early as 1895, and by Francis Penrose in 1896, 1898 and 1900 in their reports and letters on the use of iron and the preference for bronze or its alloys for the clamps between the members.

Also characteristic of Balanos' intervention was the hiding of strong reinforcements within architraves, cornice blocks and other ancient members in many cases in very ingenious ways (**Fig. 6**). This tactic, which was common in modern constructions of the era and directly opposed to the tasteless, highly visible iron bands previously employed in the earlier restorations, was well suited to Balanos' current concern for aesthetics. The result of this invasive method, however, was that in some cases the original ancient material was transformed into little more than a cover for the encasement of modern reinforcements. Such an approach caused serious, irreversible loss to the authentic material within the interior of the restored members.

In the first period of Balanos' involvement with the restoration of the Parthenon, at the end of 19th century, he was answerable to an oversight committee which controlled all the decisions. He also had several European advisors who acted as architectural consultants on his intervention, at the request of Greek authorities, although they did not closely follow Balanos' work. Among Balanos' consultants were Francis Cranmer Penrose from England, Joseph Durm from Germany and

Figure 6 Iron beam hidden in a marble beam of the Erechtheum

Lucien Magne from France, who offered advice and proposed methods, materials and principles that should have governed the intervention on the Parthenon. The German architect Wilhelm Dörpfeld was a particular influence on Balanos, especially concerning materials to be used.

The resetting of the column drums on the Parthenon's still-incomplete north side was once again raised as a matter for discussion by Durm in 1895, although Penrose and Magne were clear opponents to any such reconstruction. Despite opposition by the anti-restoration movement led primarily by Penrose, Balanos followed Durm's preference for extensive restorations and, consequently, launched his second period of intervention after 1920. At that time, an overconcentration of power and decision-making control within the person of Balanos, who proceeded to act unchecked within a cloak of authority, contributed to an entrenchment of bad restoration practises that had severe repercussions for the building.

In addition to questions of materials and extent, another issue in Balanos' Parthenon intervention, which was dealt with theoretically but never pursued practically, was the precise identification of the original positions of the monument's scattered members. The principle of restoring ancient members to their original positions was initially proposed by the French archaeologist Théophile Homolle in 1905 at the first International Congress of Archaeology in Athens after his successful experience with the *anastelosis* of the Treasury of the Athenians at Delphi. The architect Magne in a lecture at the Sorbonne also advocated the use of methods identical to those of the ancient builders – specifically, the use of dry-stone masonry joined with metal clamps. He further stated that the reconstruction of the Parthenon was only desirable if the architectural members on the ground could be identified and reset in their original positions. This view was espoused by Balanos and presented as a basic principle of his *anastelosis* programme for the north colonnade, which called for the removal of misplaced columns erected during the Pittakis restoration.

Figure 7 The restoration of an architrave of the north colonnade by Balanos in 1924. (Reproduced by kind permission of the Archaeological Society, Athens)

Restoration of the north colonnade ignited fresh debate at the 1905 Athens Congress, however, concerning the ethics of transforming ancient monuments through human interference with natural aging processes. Balanos later presented his final proposals in Rome at the 2nd International Congress of Archaeology in 1912. It was not until November 1921, however, following adverse reactions from contemporary architects, archaeologists and even poets, that he secured approval for the reconstruction of the north colonnade from the Archaeological Council of the Greek Ministry of Education. The polemic against this decision continued in the Greek and foreign press, with architect-archaeologist Anastasios Orlandos at the forefront.

The intervention on the Parthenon's north colonnade began in January 1923 and lasted until May of 1930 (**Fig.** 7). Balanos himself described the technical aspects of the intervention in his later book. The fillings of the drums were constructed of Piraeus limestone reinforced with a metal mesh encased in cement, over which he then laid a waterproof coating. The metal mesh and clamps between blocks were made of hard industrial iron. Although highly resistant to stress, this material also had a high sulphur content and was particularly sensitive to rusting that is, it had minimal resistance to moist weather conditions. Freshly cut or reused marble was employed on the upper part of the colonnade, including the column capitals, architrave blocks and triglyphs. To complete the form of partly preserved members, the broken edges of the original material was cut away to create suitable surfaces for stabilizing and joining the new marble fillings. The use of ancient marbles on Balanos' new fillings was a tactic proposed in 1894 by Penrose, who preferred to reuse members such as the fallen architraves of the north side for the repair of the west porch.

Balanos considered this practise involving marble to be very successful and had first applied it on the west porch in 1900 during his initial restoration programme. Nevertheless, in his 1940 book he defended the introduction of reinforced concrete in filling in the drums of the north colonnade. He claimed that concrete's adjustable colour allowed better aesthetic integration with the aging ancient marble. More likely, however, his choice of cement fillings for the columns was based on practical necessity. The construction of fillings from soft limestone covered with cement was much easier, faster, did not require specialised staff, and, above all, was more economical.

Balanos' intervention on the north colonnade endured many impediments, not all of them stemming from the very difficult economic conditions of the day. Some financial relief came in the form of private donations from eight American benefactors each of whom sponsored the restoration of one of the intervention's eight columns. In 1927, however, a scientific

Figure 8 The reposition of the capital of the 4th column of the north colonnade by Balanos in 1929. (Reproduced by kind permission of the Archaeological Society, Athens)

dispute almost terminated the project. During the restoration, William Bell Dinsmoor, Senior, architect of the American School of Classical Studies in Athens, noted irregularities between the restored column drums of the north colonnade and the use of unorthodox methods in the repositioning of the members. His criticisms, voiced in reports and letters, led to the work being suspended for about two years whilst a reassessment could be made of the study underlying Balanos' intervention. Dinsmoor reiterated the principles that should govern the anastelosis, finding particular fault with Balanos' identification of the original positions of the ancient members. In his extensive correspondence on the issue, discovered by Professor Fani Mallouchou in the American School archives, he outlines his disagreements with the *anastylosis* and proposes his own solution for the positions of the colonnade's drums. Balanos was ultimately forced to dismantle two already restored columns and adopt some of Dinsmoor's proposals.

Balanos restored over 200 members on the north colonnade (**Fig. 8**). His intervention lasted for nine years and was presented as an exemplary restoration at the 1931 Athens International Conference on the Restoration of Historic Monuments. This conference is also remembered for having produced the Athens Charter the first international treaty for the restoration of historic monuments. Voices critical of Balanos were also heard at this meeting, primarily regarding the materials used in his intervention, but these opposing views were diplomatically expressed as Choay mentioned in 2002 (**Fig. 9**).

The effects of corrosion of Balanos' iron reinforcements and clamps on the architectural members of the north side, have been extensively discussed in recent years. The static insufficiency of the restored members, especially of the architraves, caused by corrosion of their iron reinforcements, led the Greek Ministry of Culture and the Acropolis Restoration Service to consider new *anastelosis* works on the Parthenon's north colonnade. Although Balanos had cited the resetting of the members in their original positions as a primary goal, he was not able in practice to achieve this. The misplacement of column drums and entablature members was one of the most serious failures of his work. The negative aftermath of the

Figure 9 The north colonnade after the early 20th-century restorations by Balanos. (Photo: E. Kolyvaki, 2000, ESMA Archive)

Figure 10 The north colonnade in 2010. (Photo: S. Gesafidis, 2010)

Balanos intervention created a desire for a new approach, particularly on a technical level, planned and executed by multidisciplinary scientific teams.

2001 Intervention

The new study for the restoration of the north side of the Parthenon was approved in 1998. It was revised with new criteria and proposals for the colonnade and architraves in 2004 and for the Doric frieze and cornice in 2005. Two years later the study was further expanded to include the west edge of the Doric frieze. This extensive intervention, begun in 2001 and completed in 2009, involved the dismantling of all the architectural members previously restored by Balanos and their reassembly with some new additions for a total of 230 restored members. The method for the restoration established by the Committee for the Conservation of the Acropolis Monuments in the 1970s called for the use of Pentelic marble for the fillings and titanium rods and clamps for the reinforcements. Any ideological issue associated with a complete re-erection of this side of the Parthenon, which had collapsed three centuries earlier, was considered as resolved in 2001, since the north side in its Balanos-restored form was itself an historical entity already 70 years old.

The 2001 intervention's aim to restore and reset the fallen members on the monument in their original positions essentially represents the same objective as that of the previous restorer. The primary goal, then, was also the reconstitution of the building's original form. The intervention was considered to have been structural, since it affected not only the form but also the structure of the members by restoring their static strength. The 2001 intervention, like that of Balanos, was an extensive operation, but used totally different technological means. It posed a new set of priorities with a different approach to aesthetics. Although, the latest works made use of modern technology, just as Balanos had exploited the technology of his day, it focused on interpreting the ancient structure and on determining the static efficiency of the existing building–with the aim of insuring authenticity while improving structural integrity.

The incorporation of titanium rods into the ancient material essentially follows the previous restoration's principle of hiding reinforcements within the ancient members. The major difference between Balanos' intervention and the contemporary one, however, lies in the improved quality of

Figure 11 Misplacement of member in the Balanos restoration (each column should be one colour matching its adjacent entablature). Of a total of 185 members, 153 changed position so to be reset in their original place. (Digital drawing: P. Kostantopoulos, 2009, ESMA Archive)

modern materials and techniques. Marble was exclusively used for the new additions while titanium which studies show has an excellent compatibility with the marble was selected for the internal reinforcements. Other differences include the minimal amount of new material added to the monument and most importantly the least possible sacrifice of ancient material during the internal reinforcement of the members. That the Parthenon is being preserved as a ruin was an issue that similarly concerned Balanos, but it is also being restored to the most statically sufficient form that its remaining ancient materials allow.

The 2001 intervention was based on studies by specialist architects and civil engineers. This multi-disciplinary team drawing on an extensive set of constructional and archaeological criteria, and the results of research into the architecture and history of the monument went to great collaborative effort to solve the puzzle of the original positions of the scattered north side members in the best way possible (**Fig. 10**). It is worth noting that of the 88 column drums belonging to the 8 columns restored by Balanos, the positions of 49 drums were changed according to the new study, with 17 in agreement with Balanos' restoration, while four drum positions were in agreement with the Pittakis restoration and seven were in agreement with Dinsmoor's proposals (**Fig. 11**).

Epilogue

Restorations of the north side of the Parthenon have historically been guided by fundamental principles established more than 170 years ago, prior to any intervention on the monument, but which in practice were not always strictly followed–because of the technical necessities or limitations inherent to each era or the inability of successive restorers to manage them. The need to protect the monument's original material, preserve its historicity and respect its ruined state are concepts that have been embraced on occasion by all restorers of the Parthenon, yet with basic differences in their interpretation and practical application. In this sense, the ideological origins and language of the new priorities established for the 2001 intervention do not particularly deviate from those of Balanos, whilst also preserving the ideas of von Klenze, Magne and Homolle. Evolving theories of restoration have also affected the interventions on the Parthenon, with the incorporation of archaeological practices, and have influenced the management of practical issues on the monument. The previous, purely stylistic and aesthetic intervention on the Parthenon's north colonnade in the early 20th century has matured into a more fully developed approach with greater respect for the structure and the original material of the building.

Surface Conservation

Evi Papakonstantinou-Ziotis

Introduction

Since 1987 surface conservation of the marble of the Acropolis Monument has been closely connected to the structural restoration.

The scientific foundation for the conservation campaign was laid by the extensive research carried out at the National Technical University of Athens by the late Professor Theodor Skoulikidis and his team. There have also been multidisciplinary partnerships with universities, research institutes and scholars in other fields – including geologists, biologists and physicists. This ongoing endeavour has contributed greatly to the interpretation of decay mechanisms, design and improvement of conservation methods and materials, and to solving various problems.

The causes of decay and morphology

The main building material used for the monuments is Pentelic marble, the principal component of which is calcium carbonate. The deterioration of this marble is attributed to a combination of mechanical, physicochemical and biological factors along with atmospheric pollution, the microstructure of the marble and human interventions.The isolated or combined actions of acid rain with mechanical and biological factors, have affected the marble surface, leading to the forms of decay set out below.

Sugaring

Intergranular decohesion results in the loss of marble crystals from the surface and subsequently the loss of surface details. It is the most destructive form of decay, appearing on surface areas directly exposed to rainfall (**Fig. 1**).

Disintegration

Flaking and networks of micro-fissures appear on surface areas where the marble has less coherence, leading to rainwater penetration and retention.

Fractures and exfoliation

These are related to aluminium silicate inclusions of the marble, the destructive ancient fire, earthquakes, the explosion of 1687 and the presence of steel reinforcements used for the joining of the architectural members. Atmospheric pollutants modify the colour of the marble in sheltered places or not exposed to rainwater. Suspended particles form loose deposits and black crusts.

Biodeterioration

The presence of various micro-organisms affects the marble and the long-term effectiveness of the conservation materials. A vast variety of epilithic and chasmoendolithic microbes have been identified (such as bacteria, cyanobacteria, algae, fungi and lichens). They inflict damage through various mechanisms. Following a joint project with the Athens University Botany Department, three biocides that proved safe and effective in laboratory tests are now being tested *in situ* on the monuments in order to gauge their effectiveness (**Fig. 2**).

Failure of mortars

In addition to the damage caused by the steel and brass reinforcements, unsuitable mortars used in previous conservation projects also contributed to surface deterioration. Most mortars of this type are now flaking or powdering, thus producing soluble salts. As a result, the adjoining marble crumbles.

Deposition of suspended particles and black crusts

The formation of a black crust modifying the colour in places, not directly exposed to rainwater, increased significantly after the 1950s. The reason was the rapid industrialization of Athens. Furthermore the presence of sulphur dioxide in the atmosphere led to the formation of a gypsum layer, which up to a certain thickness preserved details of the relief (**Fig. 3**).

Figure 1 Intergranular decohesion (sugaring)

Figure 2 Biodeterioration. Chasmoendolithic microbial presence under marble surface exfoliations

Figure 3 Black crust on a Parthenon geison

Figure 4 Erechtheum, coffered ceiling of the north porch. Conservation interventions - preconsolidation

Figure 5 Conservation interventions in the Propylaea; reattachment of fragments

Figure 6 Parthenon, geison; reattachment of fragments

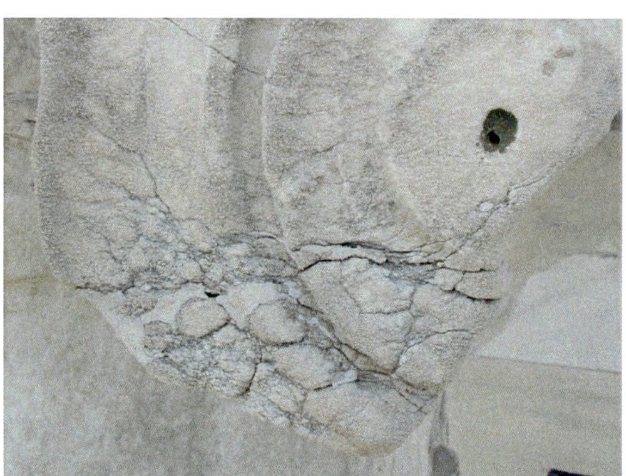

Figure 7 Erechtheum, capital K6 before conservation

Figure 8 Erechtheum, capital K6 after conservation

The conservation project

A broad-scale surface conservation project carried out by a team of qualified conservators and marble masons is currently underway on all of the Acropolis monuments (the Parthenon, the Propylaea, the Erechtheum and the Temple of Athena Nike). The interventions are both preventative-rescue and systematic in nature. All the materials used are inorganic and reversible and their physicochemical and mechanical properties are compatible with those of the aged and deteriorated marble.

Prior to the dismantling works, scattered fragments of the architectural members have to be collected and recorded. Significant finds have come to light during dismantling, for example, the *polos* and *embolion* (wooden elements used for the centering of the column drums), some of which have been very well preserved. The preventative interventions usually carried out before the removal of the architectural members also include the preconsolidation of the deteriorated surface and the 'facing' of friable or crumbling areas (**Fig. 4**). Our systematic conservation protocol for marble treatment includes the following steps (**Figs 5–8**).

Consolidation
Wherever the marble exhibits sugaring, the surface is consolidated by being sprayed or impregnated with a solution of lime (calcium hydroxide) with the addition of calcium carbonate for rapid carbonation of the material.

Removal of damaging factors
The brass pins used in previous interventions (for example, in the 60s) are removed and replaced, if need be, by new pins made of titanium. The old mortars are removed using masonry and dentistry tools.

Filling of gaps
The cracks and the interior gaps are cleaned with tools and with the use of air or de-ionized water and hydrogen peroxide. They are then filled by applying high-injectability hydraulic grouts, consisting of white Portland cement and fine-grained Pozzolano – a material similar to cement – or cement or cement-lime, according to the strength required.

Joining of fragments
The fragments that had become loose or detached from some blocks are reattached with white cement. Wherever this is considered necessary, they are reinforced with titanium dowels. When small flakes are to be attached, a reduced-strength mortar is used, consisting of cement and lime.

Sealing
Sealing the joints and the surface discontinuities comprises the final stage and its purpose is to prevent the penetration of solid particles and rainwater, as well as to smooth out the surface discontinuities. The mortar used is a cement, lime and quartz-sand mixture, with the addition of pigments (iron oxides) for chromatic harmonization with the ancient marble.

Protection
For protecting the surface from atmospheric pollution, a new material was designed. It is based on n-semiconductors and has already been applied successfully on a trial basis at the Acropolis. An artificial patina is employed in order to diminish the colour contrast between the new marble supplements and the ancient marble. This material is based on the composition of the protective material with the addition of iron oxides (**Fig. 9**).

The laser cleaning of the Parthenon west frieze
The project was the outcome of a fruitful research venture between our Service and the Institute of Electronic Structure & Laser, Foundation for Research & Technology (IESL-FORTH).

The west frieze was located above the architrave of the opisthonaos and consisted of 16 blocks depicting the beginning of the Panathenaic procession (**Fig. 10**). The first two blocks were among those parts of the temple dismantled by Lord Elgin, now on display in the British Museum.

The 14 blocks on display remained in situ until 1993, when they were removed during the restoration works carried out on the temple. Atmospheric pollution in the Attica basin over the past 50 years has resulted in severe alterations to the relief. The sculpted surface was covered by soot, other atmospheric pollutants and black crusts (**Fig. 11**).

Figure 9 Parthenon, pronaos. The artificial patina applied on new marble column capital

The cleaning project is of vital importance, since the intervention is irreversible. In addition, international experience in cleaning projects was very limited, especially when it comes to works such as Pheidias' frieze.

The aim of the project was the safe removal of the deposits, thus preserving the original surface and the details of the relief. A lengthy period of study and tests was essential for the precise diagnosis of the condition of the surface, the composition of the polluted crust and the substrate beneath and subsequently for the choice of the most suitable cleaning method. Knowledge of the composition of the polluted crust and the substrata were of great importance in choosing the cleaning method.

Two monochromatic surface layers are preserved and cover more than 30% of the surface (**Fig. 12**). These layers are distinguished in two types. The first is the lower orange-brown layer well-adhered to the marble surface. Its main components are calcium oxalates and calcium phosphates. It is described as the *epidermis* (skin) or patina encountered on many Classical and Roman monuments. The second is the outer off-white-beige layer that covers the epidermis and is described as the 'coating'. Its chemical analysis (calcium carbonate) and the brushstroke traces it bears indicate that it is a lime wash. Both of these surface layers preserve original tooling traces and relief details. Thus, they document that they form part of the original surface, and therefore, were not to be removed during the cleaning process.

The presence of sulphur dioxide in the atmosphere led to the formation of a gypsum layer, which up to a certain thickness preserves details of the relief and it should also be retained after the cleaning process. The layers of the deposits varied in thickness and composition. Their main components are gypsum, organic compounds and traces of other minerals and metals.

Figure 10 The Parthenon west frieze *in situ*. (Photo D.A.I.)

Figure 11 The dismantling of the Parthenon west frieze

Figure 12 The monochromatic surface layers, west frieze Block XVI

In terms of the substrates and the crust morphology, the following six cases could be distinguished on the west frieze surface: a) loose deposits of soot and suspended particles on the marble substrate, b) homogenous compact crust with good adhesion to the marble surface, c) dendritic crust on the marble substrate, d) loose deposits on the monochromatic surface layers, e) homogenous compact crust on the monochromatic surface layers and f) dendritic crust on the monochromatic surface layers.

Following an assessment of all the cleaning techniques currently available, four were deemed to be the most promising for further study. These were a) application of absorbent poultices, b) microblasting, c) inversion of the gypsum layer into calcite and d) laser cleaning. A research project was then carried out in order to produce a comparative study of the four cleaning techniques. The assessment of the four cleaning methods was influenced by the necessity of a gradual approach, considering the west frieze's condition. Preliminary applications of the cleaning methods were initially performed on newer marble supplements dating from the 1960s (attached to the west frieze blocks in order to replace missing parts) and which had been exposed to the same atmospheric pollution as the ancient surface. Cleaning tests then followed on representative surfaces of sculptures and architectural members of the Acropolis monuments and finally on the west frieze itself.

Quantitative and qualitative physicochemical tests were conducted to re-evaluate the effects of the four cleaning methods, both on the substrate and the black crust, before and after the cleaning process, as for example: colorimetric measurements to record the chromatic variations, observations of cross-sections under a polarizing microscope so as to examine the stratification of the substrates and the deposits, stereo microscopic observations, X Ray Diffraction and Scanning Electron Microscopy-EDAX analyses to assess the composition of the crust.

Throughout this research project, it was noted that the efficiency of the cleaning methods applied depended on the thickness and the formation of the encrustation, as well as on the type of substrates.

Following experiments, laser cleaning was selected as the method which met all the criteria for safe and effective cleaning (**Fig. 13**). It was also proven to efficiently remove all types of encrustation, without leaving any by-products on the stone surface. The laser cleaning method offered unique advantages, such as high selectivity and precision. But the most important advantage was that it was fully controllable. I should like briefly to elaborate on this. The laser cleaning method is based on the differential absorption of radiation by the substrate and the crust. The energy threshold for the removal of the superficial layer is significantly lower than that required to affect the substrate material. In particular, the energy threshold for the removal of black crust is, at 1.8 J/cm^2, about four times lower than that of the Pentelic marble, which was calculated to be 3.5 J/cm^2. This ensures the selective and self-limiting removal of the encrustation, without the slightest damage to the marble.

But we were not yet ready to proceed with the cleaning.

It has been observed that the infrared radiation, on which the commercially available laser systems are based, is effective only in some cases of encrustation. In the instances of loose deposits and homogenous compact crust on marble, the infrared laser produces a yellowing effect. On the other hand, it was also ascertained that the application of ultraviolet radiation gives the marble a greyish hue (**Fig. 14**).

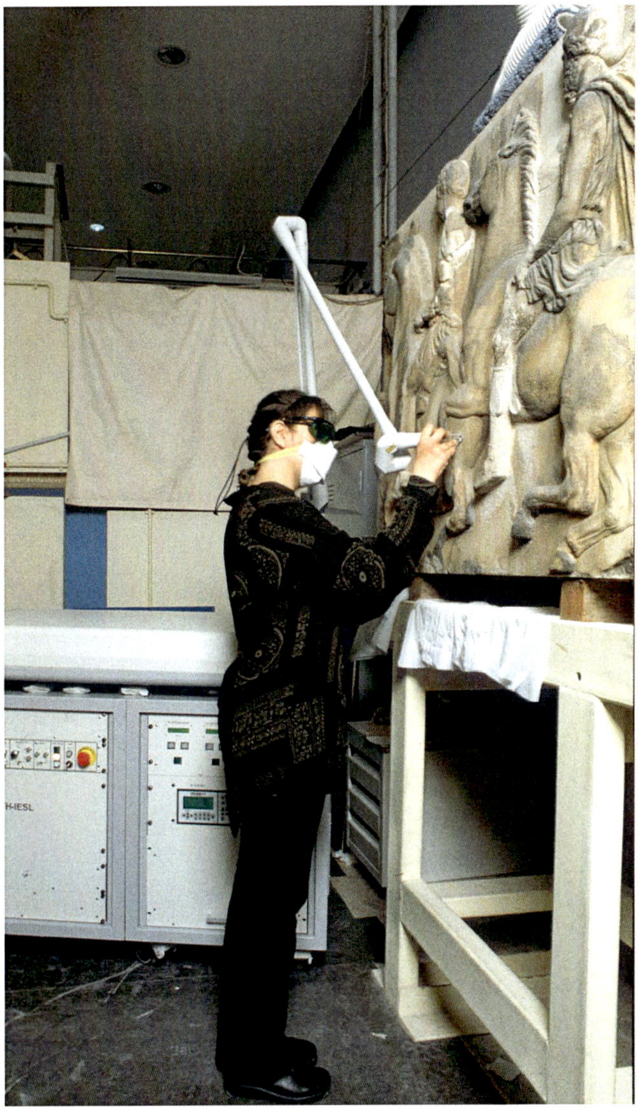

Figure 13 The laser cleaning system developed by the IESL-FORTH

Figure 14 Discolouration phenomena on the Pentelic marble caused by various laser wave lengths

Figure 15 Parthenon west frieze Block IX, before laser cleaning

Figure 16 Parthenon west frieze Block IX,after laser cleaning

Figure 17 The Parthenon west frieze Block IX, detail of traces ancient pigments revealed during the laser cleaning

Figure 18 The Parthenon west frieze Block VI, detail during cleaning

In order to avoid the yellowing effect or any other discolouration, the combined action of infrared and ultraviolet radiation was applied for the first time, with exceptional results.

Based on the above, an innovative laser system was designed and developed by the Foundation for Research and Technology-Hellas, Institute of Electronic Structure and Lasers (IESL-FORTH), especially for the west frieze. The laser system developed was a Q-switched Nd: YAG system, emitting IR and UV radiation. This hybrid system was developed with the simultaneous use of two laser beams of different wavelengths whose pulses are temporally and spatially overlapped. The energy densities of the two beams were set to a specific ratio, as determined by the preliminary tests, so as to respond to every individual case of encrustation and substrate.

The combination of the infrared and ultraviolet radiation at relatively low-energy fluences on the loose deposits was successful without any discoloration to the underlying marble surface. Combination of the infrared and ultraviolet radiation at relatively higher energy densities is also used for homogenous compact crust, with good adhesion to the marble surface. Application of the combined infrared and ultraviolet laser beams on dendritic black crust had no result at low fluences. When the fluence was increased significantly, the cleaned surface appeared rough and non-homogeneous, with visible remains of the black crust. Most acceptable results were obtained with infrared laser pulses at high-energy fluencies.

The use of ultraviolet radiation or any combination of ultraviolet and infrared radiation could cause discolouration on these layers if the substrate was monochromatic surface layers. In these cases the use of infrared radiation alone results in the acceptable cleaning of the loose deposits and the homogeneous compact crust. To remove thick dendritic crust, it was necessary significantly to increase the fluence of the applied radiation.

In conclusion, the atmospheric deposits and encrustations were removed in a controlled and safe way, while valuable details and traces of ancient colour and ancient tools were revealed during the cleaning process (**Figs 15–18**).

The cleaning project commenced in 2002 and was completed in 2004. The west frieze blocks are now on display in the New Acropolis Museum. Copies made from artificial stone were mounted in their place on the monument (**Fig. 19**).

Figure 19 The copies of the west frieze blocks on the monument

The Erechtheum project

This same laser system was transferred to the Erechtheum, where the conservation and the laser cleaning projects of the coffered-ceiling in the Porch of the Caryatids have been in progress since October 2009 (**Fig. 20**). The only traces of painted decoration that could be discerned with the naked eye (but also under magnification) were some patterns of Ionic cymation on a couple of coffer slabs and some very minute particles of blue colour (**Fig. 21**). Giovanni Verri, post-doctoral fellow at the British Museum's Department of Conservation and Scientific Research, arrived at the best possible moment. A scientific meeting was convened at the British School of Archaeology in Athens. Six speakers presented different aspects of recent discoveries of 'Egyptian Blue' on the Parthenon sulptures in Athens and London. Besides myself were Dr Christina Vlassopoulou and Mr Costas Vassiliades – archaeologist and conservator, respectively – both at the New Acropolis Museum. The British Museum was represented by Dr Ian Jenkins, Senior curator in the Department of Greece and Rome; Dr David Saunders, Keeper of the Department of Conservation and Scientific Research; and Dr Giovanni Verri, who presented his Visible-Induced Luminescense (VIL) imaging technique. We invited Giovanni Verri to the Erechtheum. This non-invasive technique developed by Verri allows us to detect and map the Egyptian blue. The method takes advantage of the very strong photo-induced infrared luminescence of this pigment. This synthetic pigment has the property of absorbing visible radiation and re-emitting infrared radiation. The emission is so strong that the luminescence can be easily imaged in a darkened room using a modified digital camera with some sensitivity in the infrared range. In the resulting greyscale images the Egyptian blue 'glows white'.

Figure 20 Erechtheum, south porch, laser cleaning of the coffers

Figure 21 Erechtheum, the south porch, coffer-slab; the visible image

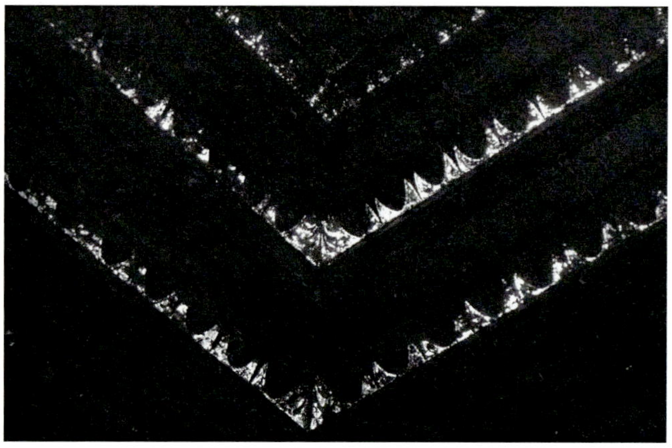

Figure 22 Erechtheum, the south porch, coffer-slab; the enhanced image

The results are impressive. In certain coffer-slabs, where we could only see minute traces of painted decoration, the method revealed the extensive presence of Egyptian blue and the details of the Ionic cymation pattern (**Figs 21, 22**). Actually, the *anthemion* patterns on the corners and the spatial distribution of every surviving particle of the pigment are also clearly discernible. In the figures we can see the visible image alongside the VIL image. We were excited by these findings. We were also happy to confirm that the laser cleaning is safe since Egyptian blue was also preserved and mapped on the cleaned areas.

In the following weeks, we obtained our own modified digital camera and appropriate equipment, and we have completed photographing the entire coffered-ceiling. The presence of Egyptian blue was subsequently confirmed using the X-Ray Diffraction (XRD) and the Scanning Electron Microscopy (SEM–EDAX) analysis methods.

It is obvious that this paves the way for revealing and mapping the lost, or rather invisible, painted decoration on all the monuments and sculptures. We now have to go back to the west frieze with this camera and look for the pigments.

I believe that this is only a sample of the secrets hidden inside the monuments that are waiting to be revealed.

The Erechtheum (1979–87)

Fani Mallouchou-Tufano

The restoration of the Erechtheum, from 1979-87 (**Fig. 1**), was the first intervention carried out on a monument of the Acropolis by the Committee for the Conservation of the Acropolis Monuments (ESMA). In this work the method, which later became the established one for all the Acropolis interventions, was for the first time applied. This consists of dismantling the parts of the monuments already restored in the past, and even some parts which, although never before dismantled, nevertheless present fissuration and fragmentation. Further, there is the conservation of the dismantled members on the ground, and their re-assembly on the monument, if possible in their original positions; finally the transferal of the architectural sculptures (in the case of the Erechtheum Caryatids) to the New Acropolis Museum and in their replacement on the monument by casts made in artificial stone.

Looking at this first *anastelosis*, with the benefit of hindsight, we see that this presents particular interest from many points of view.

For example, the Erechtheum restoration, has established the preliminary procedure which is followed prior to any intervention on the Acropolis monuments. This consists of the publication of an interdisciplinary study, comprising the comprehensive analysis of the state of preservation of the monument to be restored as well as the restoration proposals (in this particular case the 'Study for the Restoration of the Erechtheum', published in December 1977) followed by the submission of the study and of the proposals to successive assessments and approvals (first by the ESMA itself, then by international experts during intenational meetings held on the Acropolis (the first international meeting for the Erechtheum was organized on December 1977) and, finally by the Central Archaeological Council of the Ministry of Culture, which is responsible for the final decisions of intervention on the monuments. It should be noted that both the compilation of the study or the multiple control procedure (which aimed at guaranteeing the greatest possible objectivity in the decisions adopted) was at that time pioneering and innovative for Greece, a country with a long tradition in the restoration of monuments, but with a strongly personalized structure such as that dictated by Nikolaos Balanos and Anastasios Orlandos prior to 1975.

The next point to mention is that the conditions of the intervention were completely different from those current today. The works were carried out under the administrative jurisdiction of the Acropolis Ephorate with scanty and, above all, unstable financing which paid staff on a daily basis. Any work-site substructure for the execution of large scale interventions was totally missing. Hoisting loads from the outside exterior of the Acropolis to its interior was a manually operated winch of lifting capacity up to 500k, handled by eight workmen and installed at the south-east corner of the rock.

Figure 1 The Erechtheum restored. General view from south-east. (Photo: F. Mallouchou-Tufano, March 2006)

Figure 2 Transporting loads on the Acropolis plateau, in the ancient way, on rollers

Figure 4 Manual hoisting of the loads during the Erechtheum restoration

From the south-east corner the loads were transferred to the area of the Erechtheum on rollers (what the ancient Greeks called *katrakylia*), in the ancient way; **(Fig. 2)** The Acropolis Committee of the day did not approve the transport of the loads with wagons on rails. Their chief concern was to reduce any possible aesthetic interference with the rock landscape. External workshops were charged with the marble cutting. On the monument the cutting and the elaboration of the marble were done exclusively by hand with traditional tools.

For the hoisting of the loads a system of four bridge cranes on elevated rails had been chosen **(Fig. 3)**. The bridge cranes and the winches suspended by them were all manually operated **(Fig. 4)**. Once again, the Acropolis Committee had ruled out the electrical movement of the hoisting machinery. In general, the Acropolis Committee of that period was very cautious in using modern technology in the interventions. This manual execution of the work, although difficult, gave the Erechtheum restoration a character consistent with age-old traditions and practices.

The intervention on the Erechtheum began – and largely remained – a strictly rescue operation. The initial programme of the work comprised the dismantling and restoration exclusively of the parts of the monument, that had been restored in the past, and not of all of them. In the north porch for example the intervention was limited to the previously restored ceiling and did not extend below, to the parts of the columns previously restored, which were preserved in very good condition. In the course of the works, however, the very bad state of preservation of the north wall above the north entrance was revealed **(Fig. 5)**. The Acropolis Committee was forced to intervene, for the first time, on a section of the monument, which had never been dismantled, although it had been seriously disturbed by Balanos' two reinforcing bars. These were in fact the cause of the damage.

Figure 3 The Erechtheum with all the previously restored parts dismantled; general view from south-west. Visible is the system of the bridge-cranes for the hoisting of the loads

Figure 5 Dismantling the fragmented blocks of the Erechtheum north wall above the north entrance

Figure 7 Making of a new marble filling of an ancient block with the use of a pointing device

The dismantling of the previously restored parts of the monument affected the south wall up to the course of the orthostates (**Fig. 3**), the west wall to the base of the half-columns, the ceiling and the entablature of the north porch, part of the north wall down as far as the second course above the orthostates and the north-east *anta*. Approximately 720 fragmentary architectural members weighing 1 to 7 tons had been dismantled, amounting to about 1,250 tons in total. The Caryatids were transferred to the Acropolis Museum and replaced on the monument by casts.

The restoration of the north-east corner of the monument was from the beginning included in the restoration project. This intervention was considered necessary for the static improvement of the monument against the horizontal force of wind as well as seismic action and also for the recovery of the integrity of the form of the eastern, main, facade of the monument, which had been reduced by Lord Elgin's actions. In the course of the work the material used for the replacement of missing architectural members was established: artificial stone for the replacement, by casts, of architectural members preserved outside the monument (the north-east column in the British Museum), natural stone, identical to the one used at the initial construction, for the replacement of architectural members altogether lost.

The materials and the techniques of intervention were for the first time applied and tested, in the restoration of the Erechtheum and were later to become standard in the Acropolis restoration project.

For the first time in the history of building conservation anywhere in the world, titanium was used in the restoration of a monument. Titanium was used for joining either the fragments of the ancient members together, or the new marble fillings with the ancient members. The joining of the fragments of the architectural members was formerly done in a vertical

Figure 6 Vertical joining of the fragments of a west wall engaged column with titanium rods

Figure 8 Setting a new marble filling on the blocks of the south wall under the orthostates. Visible in the centre is the foreman of the marble technicians N. Skarris

way (**Fig. 6**). This obsolete technique has now been abandoned and the fragments of the members are joined horizontally in specially designed movable tables. During the Erechtheum intervention the use of the pointing device in the fabrication of the new marble fillings of the ancient blocks was also used for the first time (**Fig. 7**). This is the device through which a surface is formed in negative to the broken surface of the ancient block, insuring thus the reversible filling of the ancient member (**Fig. 8**).

Titanium was also used to replace the metallic elements of the previous interventions. This affected both the clamps and dowels and the bigger metal reinforcements, such as the structure inserted in the interior of the architraves of the porch of the Caryatids or the big iron beams, from which the marble beams of the ceiling of the north porch had been suspended. In using the titanium, especially as far as structural reinforcement is concerned, the solutions set forth by Balanos were faithfully repeated, although in some cases these solutions did not take full advantage of the new material's full potential. As far as concerns the new titanium reinforcement of the Caryatid Porch. Shaped in the form of the letter Π of the Greek alphabet, it is identical to the older one set in the interior of the architraves of the porch (**Fig. 9**) with vertical supports that transfer the weight of the ceiling to the podium. These relieve the Caryatids from the weight of the structure above. The only difference between the earlier and later interventions is that the vertical supports are now concealed inside the casts of the Caryatids, thus aesthetically enhancing the porch (**Fig. 10**). An identical titanium bar also replaced the older iron one above and along the architraves of the west wall of the Erechtheum (**Fig. 11**). Behind the lintel of the north entrance, however, a sole titanium beam replaced the two iron beams placed there during Balanos' restoration.

During the joining of the members new titanium clamps and dowels have been used (**Fig. 12**). The horizontal clamps are of various dimensions and shapes. They replace joining elements of four types that derive from the original construction phase of the monument and the subsequent three interventions, that of Roman times, that of the mid-19th and that of the beginning of the 20th centuries. In order to avoid further cutting of the ancient pieces, the extant sockets, that is the cavities in which the clamps and dowels are placed, have been re-used to insert a suitable joining element. The profiles of the new joining elements, as well as their proportional and dimensional relation to the sockets and the thickness of the cement compound that covers them, have been particularly studied during the fabrication of the joining elements and their placement in the monument. All these were completely original technological innovations at the time. The specially developed cement compound around the joining elements, ensuring the best behaviour of the joining elements, was used in the sealing for the new titanium elements instead of lead as in antiquity.

In the restoration of the Erechtheum for the first time the Balanos restoration practices which are contrary to today's restoration ethics have been corrected. These are the erroneous and random positioning of the monument's architectural members during their re-assembly and the practice of creating architectural blocks that could be restored by 'stitching them together' from various ancient fragments of various origins. In 1982 C. Zambas, the civil engineer in charge of the restoration,

Figure 9 The new titanium structure in the interior of the architraves of the Erechtheum south porch

Figure 10 The Erechtheum south porch after restoration with the cast copies of the Caryatids; view from south

Figure 11 The new titanium rod above and along the west wall of the Erechtheum

Figure 12 New titanium clamps for the joining of the orthostates of the Erechtheum south porch podium

Figure 13 The Erechtheum north porch and wall after restoration. Reinserted in the wall are the 23 blocks, which in a previous intervention, had been used in the restoration of the south wall

first systematically investigated the correct position of the blocks of the south wall of the monument. This pioneering study opened the way to researches in that direction and set up the relevant methodology. In 1985 a corresponding study for the re-assembly of the blocks of the north wall was undertaken by A. Papanikolaou, the architect in charge and director of the whole restoration operation of the Erechtheum. In this way, during their restoration the lateral walls of the cella of the monument recaptured both their original structure and their structural inclinations. During the re-assembly, 23 blocks of the north wall, that had been used for the restoration of the south wall, returned to their original position; the opposite happened for 6 blocks of the south wall (**Fig. 13**). The gaps that resulted from the removal and transposing of the members have been filled with completely new blocks made out of new Pentelic marble. Furthermore, through the repositioning of the blocks and the recovery of their original positions, the original sockets of the joining elements have been also recaptured and re-used. In some cases, in order to be re-used, the edges of the sockets, destroyed in the past during the violent extraction of the metal joining elements, had to be filled with new marble. The irrelevant ancient fragments that had been used in the past to fill in the blocks of the lateral walls of the Erechtheum have now been removed and replaced by new Pentelic marble.

In the west wall of the Erechtheum, which had been recomposed in a pastiche way by Balanos, the identification of the original location of the blocks has not been possible. Thus, during the new restoration, only the rusted iron joining elements of the previous intervention were replaced by others of titanium, while Balanos' arrangement of the blocks of the wall was followed. In this case Balanos' recomposed blocks of the wall were retained. Only in some cases, where the creation of a better bedding surface for the superimposed course has been judged necessary, have the blocks been filled with new marble.

The original positioning and sequence of the architectural members has been recovered in other parts of the monument as well, as, for example the crown course of the podium of the Caryatid porch or in the coffered ceiling of the north porch. In other cases however, as, for example, in the entablature of the north porch or the *epicranitis* (or crowning) course of the south wall, the older arrangement has been kept. In some cases a course in which the original structure has been recovered meets another one, which follows the previous restorer's arrangement: this is the case, for example, in the meeting of the second-from-top course of the south wall, in which the original structure had been recovered, with the *epicranitis* course above. In these cases the problem that arose by the lack of coincidence between the sockets of the dowels in the vertical joining of the blocks was solved with the use of specially designed joining elements, (in the case of the two upper courses of the south wall S-shaped dowels have been used) (**Fig. 14**).

Finally, during the restoration of the Erechtheum, one of the most complex problems of the Acropolis monuments restoration has been dealt with: the restoration of the inner

Figure 14 S-shaped dowels, specifically designed, used for the joining of the restored two upper courses of the Erechtheum south wall

faces of the walls of the monuments seriously damaged by fire. The missing portions cause great problems as far as the stability of the monuments is concerned. Thus, during the intervention in the Erechtheum the orthostates of the lateral walls of the cella of the monument have been restored, for structural reasons, to their original thickness. Some other blocks also, in the upper parts of the walls, have been filled in with new marble in order to ameliorate their structural capacity. Depending on the individual cases, the surface of the new stone was given a final or semi-final treatment to match better to the adjacent ancient blocks. Likewise, both for stability and for didactic considerations, part of the inner, transversal wall of the monument was restored (**Fig. 15**).

No retelling of the restoration of the Erechtheum would be complete without a mention of those who contributed most to it: First of all, the three founding members of the Acropolis Committee, Professors Charalambos Bouras, Sokrates Aggelidis and Theodore Skoulikidies, who guided and supervised the inexperienced, then, young engineers in charge of the work. Secondly, the engineers in charge of the work, the late Alekos Papanikolaou, architect (**Fig. 16**), and the civil engineer Kostas Zambas. Despite their youth, in an exemplary collaboration they dealt with all the problems that emerged and brought to an end a pioneering project in its time. Finally, I should recall the most valuable contributors, the marble technicians (**Fig. 17**). They belonged to three generations: some senior technicians who had already worked on the big scale restoration interventions on ancient monuments in Greece of the post-war period (the 1950s and 60s) ; some younger, but experienced technicians, who had occasionally worked on monuments; finally young technicians, who had just finished training at the Technical School for marble cutting on the island of TInos, who are the foremen to the interventions of today on the Acropolis. Among them Nikolaos Skarris, the foreman of the crew, was distinguished for his character and above all for his incomparable skill (**Fig. 8**).

Figure 15 The interior face of the restored Erechtheum south wall; view from north-west

Figure 16 Transferring the 6th Caryatid to the Acropolis Museum. Visible on the right Alekos Papanikolaou, architect in charge of the work

Figure 17 Restoring the dismantled wall blocks of the Erechtheum on the Acropolis plateau

Above all the restoration of the Erechtheum was carried out within a unique atmosphere immediately after the fall of the military dictatorship (in 1974), when a unique sense of collectivity, optimism and great expectations prevailed throughthout the whole of Greece. It was executed by young scholars, inexperienced but enthousiastic and was characterized by skilled handicraft of a kind found in antiquity. As Evi Touloupa, Ephor of the Acropolis during most of the project, has written in 2001:

> It is a delight to see today a host of new technicians working with ultra modern technical equipment and the supervision of many well-qualified engineers and archeologists. Yet, the sight of the shed, the sounds of the hammer, the whole atmosphere as it was around the Erechtheum took us back more closely to the time when the Acropolis monuments were built, took us closer to the years of Pheidias (**Fig. 18**).

Figure 18 The marble technicians of the Erechtheum restoration during the removal of the copy of the 3rd Caryatid

Bibliography

Balanos, N. 1940. *The Restoration of the Acropolis Monuments*, Athens (in Greek).

Balanos, N. 1938. *Les monuments de l'Acropole, relèvement et conservation*, Paris.

Bouras, Ch. 1977. 'Pour sauver l' Acropole', *Courier de l'UNESCO*, 4–10.

Bouras, Ch. 1984. 'Athens. The Parthenon', *Monumentum* 27/2, Athens, 109–120.

Bouras, Ch. 1985. 'The program of the preservation of the monuments of the Athenian Acropolis', *Actes du XIIe Congrès International d'Archéologie classique*, Athènes 4–10 septembre 1983, Athens, 361–365.

Bouras, Ch. 1993. 'Monuments of the Antiquity. The limits of restoration', *Actes du Congrès International sur la conservation de la pierre*, Paris, 127–130.

Bouras, Ch. 1994. 'Restoration work on the Parthenon, and changing attitudes towards the conservation of monuments', in P. Tournikiotis (ed.), *The Parthenon and its Impact in Modern Times*, Athens, 310–339.

Bouras, Ch. and K. Zambas, 2002. *The Works on the Acropolis of Athens*, C. Hadziaslani (ed.), Athens.

Casanaki, M. and F. Mallouchou-Tufano, 1983. *The Acropolis at Athens Conservation, Restoration and Research (1975–1983)*, Athens.

Cavvadias, P. 1905. 'La question de la restauration des monuments et en particulier, du Parthénon', *Comptes rendus du Congrès International d'Archéologie*, 1ère session 7–13 avril (25–31 mars), Athens, 245–247.

Choay F. (ed.) 2002. *La Conference d' Athènes sur la conservation artistique et historique des monuments* (1931), Paris.

Cipriani M. 2004 . *Il Restauro dei Templi di Poseidonia*, Paestum.

Dontas, G. 1976. 'Probleme der Restaurierung und Erhaltung der Acropolis', *Archäologie und Denkmalpflege* 2, Berlin, 111–118.

Economakis, R. (ed.) 1994. *Acropolis Restoration, the CCAM Interventions*, London.

Filetici, M.G., F. Giovanetti, F. Mallouchou-Tufano and E. Pallotino (eds) 2003. *Restoration of the Athenian Acropolis (1975–2003)*, Quaderni ARCo, Rome.

Genovese R.A. (ed.) 1985. *L'Acropoli di Atene, Conservazione e restauro*, Naples.

Giraud, D. 1994. *Study for the Restoration of the Temple of Athena Nike*, 2 vols, Athens (in Greek).

Hadziaslani, C., E. Kaïmara and A. Leonti, 2011. *Acropolis and Education*, Athens (in Greek).

Homolle, T. 1905. *'Le Trésor des Athéniens à Delphes', Comptes rendus du Congrès International d'Archéologie, 1ére session 7–13 avril (25-31 mars)*, Athens, 167–71.

Cipriani, M. and G. Avagliano (eds) 2007. *Il restauro dei templi di Poseidonia, Un intervento di conservazione e valorizzazione*, Atti del Convegno Internationale, Paestum 26–27 giugno 2004 (esp. 103–180).

Ioannidou, M. 2002. 'The restoration work on the Acropolis from 1975 until today.' *Corpus, Archeology in Greece*, special issue, Athens 110–115 (in Greek).

Ioannidou, M. 2005. 'The restoration of the Acropolis monuments: An intervention in close relationship with research which takes advantage of the modern technology'. *Research and Technology*, January 2005, 35–8 (in Greek).

Ioannidou, M. 2007. *The Restoration of the Propylaia of the Athenian Acropolis*. Athens.

Ioannidou M. 2007. 'Principles and methodology of intervention for structural restoration', *Proceedings of the XXI International Symposium CIPA 2007 Anticipating the Future of the Cultural Past*, Athens 376–381.

Ioannidou, M. and E. Lebidaki (eds) 2011. *The Restoration of the Monuments of the Athenian Acropolis*. 2nd edition, Athens

Irwin, D. (ed.) 1972. *Winckelmann Writing on Art*, London.

Jokilehto J. 1986. 'A history of architectural conservation: The contribution of English, French German and Italian thought towards an international approach to the conservation of cultural property', D.Phil thesis, York 1986, recomposed in PDF format, February 2005, www.iccrom.org/pdf/ICCROM_05_HistoryofConservation00_en.pdf.

Jokilehto, J. 1999. *A History of Architectural Conservation*, Oxford.

Klenze, L. von 1838. *Aphoristische Bemerkungen gesammelt auf seiner Reise nach Griechenland*, Berlin.

Kokkou A. 1977. *The Provision of the Antiquities in Greece and the First Museums*, Athens (in Greek).

Korres, M. and Ch. Bouras, 1983. *Study for the Restoration of the Parthenon*, vol. 1, Athens (in Greek).

Korres, M., N. Toganidis, K. Zambas and Th. Skoulikidis 1989. *Study for the Restoration of the Parthenon*, vol. 2a, Athens (in Greek).

Korres, M. 1989. *Study for the Restoration of the Parthenon*, vol. 2b, Athens (in Greek).

Korres, M. 1991. *Contribution to the Study of the Structural Form of the Ancient Columns*, Doctoral thesis, Athens (in Greek).

Korres, M. 1994. *Study for the Restoration of the Parthenon*, vol. 4. Athens (in Greek).

Korres, M. 1995. *From Pentelicon to the Parthenon*, Athens.

Koufopoulos, P. 1994. *Study for the Restoration of the Parthenon*, vol. 3a. Athens (in Greek).

Mallouchou-Tufano, F. 1998. *The Restoration of Ancient Monuments in Modern Greece, 1834–1939*. Athens (in Greek).

Mallouchou-Tufano, F. 2006a. 'Thirty years of anastelosis work on the Athenian Acropolis 1975–2005', *Conservation and Management of Archaeological Sites* 8:1, 27–38.

Mallouchou-Tufano, F. 2006b. 'The restoration of classical monuments in modern Greece: historic precedents, modern trends, peculiarities', *Conservation and Management of Archaeological Sites* 8:3, 154–173.

Mallouchou-Tufano, F. and Y. Alexopoulos, 2007. 'Digital management of the documentation of the Acropolis restoration', *Proceedings of the XXI International Symposium CIPA 2007 Anticipating the future of the cultural past*, Athens, 475–9.

Papageorgiou-Venetas A. 2000. *Leo von Klenze in Greece*, Athens.

Papakonstantinou, E., K. Frantzikinaki, P. Pouli and B. Zafyropoulos, 2002. *The Parthenon West Frieze: a Study of Cleaning Methods*. Athens (in Greek).

Papanikolaou, A. 1984. Wedge-like opening in the Erechtheion, *Archaeologikon Deltion* 23, A' 191–198, (in Greek).

Papanikolaou, A. 2004. 'The project concerning the conservation and restoration of the Erechteum', in *Ergon* 114, *Restoration of Monuments, Rehabilitation of Historical Buildings in Attika*, J. Kizis (ed.), 28–49 (in Greek with an English summary).

Paraschis, C. and N. Toganidis, 2002. *Study for the Restoration of the South Wall of the Parthenon*, Athens (in Greek).

Petrakos, V. 1987. *History of the Archaeological Society of Athens 1837–1987*, Athens.

Petropoulou, E. 2008. 'Restoration and the public: Results of a visitors' survey on the restoration of the Acropolis monuments', *Conservation and Management of Archaeological Sites* 10:2, 132–156.

Proceedings, 2nd International Meeting for the Restoration of the Acropolis Monuments, 1985, F. Mallouchou-Tufano (ed.), Athens.

Proceedings, of the 3nd International Meeting for the Restoration of the Acropolis Monuments, 1990, Ch. Vlassopoulou (ed.), Athens.

Proceedings, of the 4nd International Meeting for the Restoration of the Acropolis Monuments, 1995, F. Mallouchou-Tufano (ed.), Athens.

Proceedings, of the 5nd International Meeting for the Restoration of the Acropolis Monuments, 2002. F. Mallouchou-Tufano (ed.), Athens.

Bibliography

Study for the Restoration of the Erechtheion, 1977, Collective work, Athens (in Greek).

Skoulikidis, Th., E. Papakonstantinou, A. Galanos and J. Doganis, 1994. *Study for the Restoration of the Parthenon* vol. 3c, Athens (in Greek).

Skoulikidis, Th., 2002. *Methods of Conservation of Pentelic Marble,* Athens (in Greek).

Tanoulas, T. 1987. 'The Propylaea of the Acropolis at Athens since the seventeenth century' *Jahrbuch des Deutschen Archäologischen Instituts* 102, 413–83.

Tanoulas, T. 1997. *'The Propylaia of the Athenian Acropolis from AD 267 to 1458'*, Athens.

Tanoulas, T. 1998. 'A' ephory of Prehistoric and Classical antiquities. Restoration works. Propylaia', *Archaiologikon Deltion* 53, B' I', 30–6, pls 18–22.

Tanoulas, T. 2006a. 'About clamps and dowels at the central building of the Propylaia of the Athenian Acropolis' in *Ancient Greek Technology, Proceedings 2nd International Conference,* Athens, 448–56.

Tanoulas, T. 2007b. 'La restauration des Propylées', *Patrimoines, revue de l'Institut national du patrimoine*, 3, 62–9.

Tanoulas, T., M. Ioannidou and A. Moraitou, 1994. *Study for the Restoration of the Propylaia*, Athens (in Greek).

Tanoulas, T., M. Ioannidou, 2002. *Study for the Restoration of the Superstructure of the Central Building of the Propylaia,* Athens (in Greek).

The Acropolis Restoration News (Newsletter of the Acropolis Restoration Service) vols 1–11 (2001–2011), Athens.

Toganidis, N. 1994. *Study for the Restoration of the Parthenon,* vol. 5, Athens (in Greek).

Travlos, J. 1971. *Pictorial Dictionary of Ancient Athens*, London.

Varoufakis G., 1992. 'How did the iron clamps of the temples of the Acropolis resist rusting', *Archaeologia* 45, 14–19.

Working group for the preservation of the Acropolis Monuments, 1977. *International Meeting on the Restoration of the Erechteum. Reports, Proposals, Conclusions.* Athens.

Zambas K., M. Ioannidou and A. Papanikolaou, 1986. 'The use of titanium reinforcement for the restoration of marble architectural members of the Acropolis monuments'. *Case Studies in the Conservation of Stone and Wall Buildings,* IIC Congress, Bologna, 138–141.

Zambas, K. 1994. *Study for the Restoration of the Parthenon*, vol. 3b Athens (in Greek).

Zambas, K. 2002. 'The refinements of the columns of the Parthenon'. Phd thesis, Athens (in Greek).

Zambas, K. 2002. *Study for the Restoration of the North Colonnade of the Parthenon,* Athens (in Greek).